Transforming Criminal Policy

Spheres of Influence

in

The United States, The Netherlands and
England and Wales during the 1980s

Andrew Rutherford

Waterside Press Criminal Policy Series Volume I
Series Editor Andrew Rutherford

Transforming Criminal Policy

Published 1996 by
WATERSIDE PRESS
Domum Road
Winchester SO23 9NN
Telephone or Fax 01962 855567

ISBN Paperback 1 872 870 31 7

Cataloguing-in-publication data A catalogue record for this work can be obtained from the British Library.

Waterside Press Criminal Policy Series Volume I

Cover design John Good Holbrook Ltd, Coventry

Printing and binding Antony Rowe Ltd, Chippenham

In Memory of Margaret Spurway

1905-1994

Preface and Acknowledgments

In exploring the transformation of criminal policy in three Western countries, the focus of this study is upon the influences exerted by strategically placed individuals. The underlying tensions of purpose and direction and the relative weight attached to competing values are among the driving forces of the transformation process, and the omens for the latter 1990s and into the next century provide little solace for those who stress the human rights dimension of criminal policy.

Criminal policy-making ought to be a matter of rational and truthful argument, and those people who are closest to these issues carry the responsibility for engaging in the wider public debate. Margaret Spurway, to whom this book is dedicated, devoted her life to training teachers and would happily challenge the assertions of specialists in many fields, including this one. Criminal policy is too important to be left to the experts, but clearly, it cannot be shaped by referenda. Ways must be found to more adequately inform the spheres of influence which shape any society's response to crime.

Many people have made this book possible. Special mention should be made of the members and staff of the National Criminal Justice Commission who have had, over the last two years, the awesome task of attempting to alter the disastrous course of policy in the United States. My fellow European on the Commission, Nils Christie, has been a particular source of inspiration. The international conference on Prison Growth, which he organized in April 1995, provided me with the encouragement to complete this project. I have also greatly benefited from many discussions with René van Swaaningen of Erasmus University Rotterdam. Two of his students, Dorine Peters and

Angenita Pex were careful and well informed translators, as was Daphne Ahrendt, a graduate student at the London School of Economics. Generous financial support was provided by the Barrow and Geraldine S Cadbury Trust and by the research committee of the Law Faculty at Southampton University. I was most efficiently served by the research assistance of James Harvey and by the clerical support of Careen Tompkins. As always the text has been immeasurably improved by the keen eye and loving support of Judith Rutherford.

Andrew Rutherford
Southampton
November, 1995

Transforming Criminal Policy

CONTENTS

WINCHESTER

CHAPTER 1

Shaping Criminal Policy

It has become commonplace to think about crime in narrow and compartmentalised ways. All too often, when policy is mentioned it is prefixed by expressions such as 'law and order', 'anti-crime' or 'crime control'. The narrow lens implied by these conventional terms places certain issues at the top of the policy agenda, while others remain excluded from consideration. Policy solely as an instrument to combat crime has immediate appeal, and it has become especially seductive in recent times because of its populist simplicity. For these reasons, narrow perspectives of this sort have become all the more difficult to challenge. Philip Heymann, when he resigned in February 1994 as United States Deputy Attorney General, remarked that it

> had been too easy to pretend that we're going to solve the problem of crime with a set of remedies that look good for about the first fifteen seconds and look worse as you get to the half minute . . . The problem here is that this whole area is so much a matter of political debate that there is no room for reasoned debate.[1]

But a broad and integrated criminal policy which recognises the crucial political and philosophical issues at stake does not lend itself to a series of pronouncements by 'soundbite', and instead demands the time and attention required for what Thomas Mathiesen calls 'communicative rationality'.[2]

Criminal policy, when defined broadly, may be said to include 'the whole of society's specific response to the problems posed by the phenomenon of crime'.[3] Defined in this way, criminal policy serves as an ideal framework, the core aspects of which include determinations as to the limits of the criminal law (including personal responsibility); the measures taken to combat crime at every stage of the criminal justice process; the protections afforded to individuals from arbitrary stop, search and arrest and which also provide fair, just and decent treatment thereafter; the evenhandedness of the administration of the criminal law without regard to gender, class and ethnicity; the status of the victims of crime; and finally, the far-reaching and multi-faceted arena of crime prevention.[4]

11

There are also dangers in taking too broad a sweep and thereby blurring the boundary between criminal policy and social policy generally. For example, an official Swedish agency has stated that criminal policy applies 'to all measures undertaken to limit criminal behaviour. It refers not only to the activities of the police, the courts of justice or the prison and probation system, but also to *social policy reforms* concerning the labour market, schools, housing and town planning or social life.'[5] It follows from this definition that any social policy which reduces crime falls within the ambit of criminal policy, which is not only conceptually absurd, but carries with it all the dangers of intrusive intervention by the state. A more sensible approach is to explicitly recognise what one expert on urban issues has called the neglected 'noncrime' public policies such as housing, families and child development.[6] In exploring recent developments in three countries, this book's central theme is an insistence upon integrated criminal policy as a means of protecting those values which are fundamental to a liberal democracy. But criminal policy is never going to be tidy, coherent or cohesive. As a leading German criminologist has caustically observed: 'Whoever believes that today's criminal policy debate can be reduced to a single streamlined formula has not understood what he or she is talking about.' Above all, criminal policy should be seen as a dynamic process which is 'a very colourful mosaic, which is not static but a moving picture'.[7]

This untidy and unsettled state of affairs reflects the ad hoc and fragmented nature of much of the activity which takes place. After all, there are often powerful and principled rationales for this fragmentation. But does criminal policy really amount to more than the amalgam of disparate and competing strands which co-exist within a state of uncertain resolution? Questions of this sort may reflect doubts as to whether the idea of criminal policy itself is to be welcomed. For example, the distinguished Dutch criminal lawyer, Auguste 't Hart, has remarked: 'The notion that it is possible to pursue a specific criminal law policy is fostered in the Dutch situation by the pretence that, given the form of organization in The Netherlands, there is ample opportunity to coordinate and rationalize detection and prosecution work.'[8] But 't Hart's invaluable critique of contemporary developments in The Netherlands is itself testimony to the importance of entering the fray and not leaving the running to those who would take criminal policy in a narrow direction.

Criminal policy-making can never be constructed on new foundations. Even within states which have emerged from the former Soviet bloc, much 'baggage' has been carried forward by historical

12

attitudes and traditional arrangements.[9] Nor can criminal policy-making be divorced from the wider political context or protected from the immediate press of events, expected and otherwise. As Paul Rock has commented, policy-making 'would be an otherwise smooth metamorphosis were it not for the sudden lurches and opportunities imposed by uncontrollable problems of timing and context.'[10]

However, opportunities do arise which enable fundamental questions to be raised about future directions. The start of any such endeavour, as Andrew Ashworth has insisted with regard to criminal justice, must be from a 'principled basis'. The primary question, he suggests, 'is not *whether* the criminal justice system should be reshaped, or even *how* it should be reshaped, but *on what basis* it should be re-shaped.'[11]

At the core of this question are issues concerning the relative weight to be given to the instrumental and normative objectives of criminal policy. Many commentators agree that criminal policy has come to be increasingly driven by an instrumental agenda, with crime control objectives to the fore. As Nicola Lacey has argued, instrumentalism 'diverts attention away from contested political questions about what constitutes value in the relevant context, and from pressing questions about how these values should be debated and determined . . .'[12] In a similar vein, Antonie Peters has written of a 'pervasive instrumentalism (becoming) the frameless frame of official action, no longer contained by legal norms and constitutional principles.'[13] But are there not circumstances in which the human rights dimension should be afforded at least as much weight as instrumental considerations? It is essential to this dimension that fundamental protections of the individual be built into the substantive criminal law , its procedures and administration, but this imperative is sometimes neglected even by those who might be expected to afford it the most prominence. For example, it has been argued that liberal reformers in the United States gave undue priority to an 'administrative strategy' over a 'rights strategy' in tackling the inequities of bail decision-making, which had the unintended consequence of reducing the rights of the defendant.[14] Only with an integrated criminal policy are normative concepts such as legality, the rule of law and considerations of basic humanity, likely to be adequately protected and expressed.

Individuals can and do make a difference to the on-going transformation of criminal policy, even though their activities often remain at the margins. This study explores the influence exerted by three people within the context of developments in the United States,

The Netherlands and England and Wales during the 1980s. Within each of these three countries governments to the right of the political spectrum were in control, but there were strong indications that political parties to the left had become increasingly shy of a principled approach to criminal policy. There were also growing public anxieties that the crime problem was worsening, and Leon Radzinowicz may well be correct in asserting that this 'crime pressure' inevitably leads to a 'crystallisation of public opinion against measures of criminal policy inspired by a liberal social outlook and a gravitation towards short-cut solutions usually identified with authoritarian systems of criminal justice.'[15] Public anxiety about crime, along with the increasingly politicised nature of criminal policy and concerns about escalating costs incurred by the various agencies have combined to encourage central governments to seek greater influence, if not control, over the largely decentralized activities of criminal justice and crime prevention. In short, the role of central government has extended beyond defining the scope and substance of the criminal law, increasingly reaching into areas which traditionally have been regarded as the preserve of local political structures.

These general themes notwithstanding, certain developments have followed a distinctive national course. In the United States the most notable feature has been the unprecedented escalation in the use of imprisonment at the local, state and federal levels of government. The number of prisoners measured as a rate of national population had remained remarkably stable over the fifty years up to the early 1970s. But from the mid-1970s the number of people held in prisons and jails began to rise, and escalated through the 1980s with particular ferocity, with the imprisonment rate rising threefold by 1990. By sharp contrast, during the latter 1980s the pattern of criminal justice in England and Wales was in some respects one of de-escalation and was marked by a fall in the prison population at the end of the decade. Indeed, it was a paradox of Mrs Thatcher's third administration that criminal policy moved (to use the scheme developed by Radzinowicz)[16] from a 'conservative' model in the direction of being a 'socio-liberal' model. As a further illustration of the unexpected, the 'socio-liberal' model no longer seemed to enjoy its natural home in The Netherlands. Instead, as two close observers have noted, at the discursive level there was an increasingly moralistic law and order rhetoric, whereas actual policy developments were characterized by a form of planned justice, 'in which the principles of due process are gradually replaced by a management approach of an efficient procedural order and where

14

even the quality of the rule of law is interpreted in terms of organizational efficiency.'[17]

This study is not a comprehensive comparative analysis of the dynamics of criminal policy-making, but has the more modest purpose of raising questions about how criminal policy was influenced through the professional activities of three remarkable individuals. Each occupied a distinct strategic vantage point with its own constraints, and worked within a particular sphere of influence. In the United States, James Q Wilson was without parallel among academic commentators in articulating and legitimizing a hard-edged approach to criminal policy. His book, *Thinking About Crime*, published in 1975, caught the turn of the political tide and made an immediate and enormous impact, becoming at once the standard rebuttal to the liberal criminal policy vision exemplified by President Johnson's Crime Commission. Wilson's public profile continued to rise throughout the Reagan and Bush administrations, and his prolific publishing and numerous advisory roles have ensured that he remains a very considerable presence on the American criminal policy scene.

In The Netherlands, a key figure in challenging the traditionally mild and tolerant criminal policy has been Dato Steenhuis. A very senior prosecutor who has also held top research posts within the Ministry of Justice, Steenhuis was a central player in efforts to give criminal policy more public credibility. The strident managerialism propagated by Steenhuis did much to displace the liberal humanitarianism which had long characterized this area of public policy. In England and Wales, the senior official responsible for criminal policy throughout the decade was David Faulkner. In working closely with ministers and within the constraints incumbent upon a senior civil servant, Faulkner used his considerable skills to give shape and vision to criminal policy. Against the background of the preoccupations, perceptions and ideological cross-currents of three Thatcher administrations, he took advantage of events and opportunities so as to articulate the direction of policy and to move matters forward. The multifarious influences which determined the flow of criminal policy during the 1980s included the activities of these three strategically well-placed individuals, each of whom had a definite vision as to its eventual course.

15

ENDNOTES

1. Philip Heymann, quoted in *The New York Times* (16 February, 1994).

2. Thomas Mathiesen, 'Contemporary Penal Policy: A Study in Moral Panics', (lecture to the Annual General Meeting of the Howard League for Penal Reform, London, 25 November, 1992), 10-11; Mathiesen acknowledges that the term was first used by the German sociologist, Jürgen Habermas.

3. Michael Moriarty, 'The Policy-Making Process: how it is seen from the Home Office', in Nigel Walker (ed), *Penal Policy-Making in England* (Cambridge, Cambridge Institute of Criminology, 1977), 144.

4. The term 'criminal policy' subsumes but extends beyond the realms of 'penal policy' and 'criminal justice'. Nor is criminal policy synonymous with 'politique criminelle' which has been defined as 'the concern to re-orientate society's reaction to crime by bringing to bear the resources and methods of criminology and a better understanding of the evolution of the institutions and ideas concerning the prevention and repression of crime'. Marc Ancel, 'The relationship between criminology and "Politique Criminelle"', in Roger Hood (ed), *Crime, Criminology and Public Policy Essays in Honour of Sir Leon Radzinowicz* (London, Heinemann, 1974), 269; The term 'law enforcement', despite its conventional narrow usage, does at least pay heed to issues such as the protection of individual rights; see especially Auguste 't Hart's exploration of 'enforcement of the law'. Auguste C 't Hart, *Openbaar Ministerie en Rechtshandhaving, een verkenning* [Public Prosecution and Law Enforcement, An Exploration] (Arnhem, Gouda Quint, 1994).

5. National Council for Crime Prevention, *Crime and Criminal Policy in Sweden 1985*, Report No 19, (Stockholm, National Council for Crime Prevention, 1985), 5; emphasis added; for a critique of a broad approach to criminal policy by the Norwegian government in the late 1970s, see Thomas Mathiesen, 'The Future of Control Systems - the Case of Norway' in David Garland and Peter Young (eds) *The Power to Punish* (London, Heinemann Educational Books, 1983), 130-145.

6. Robert J Sampson, 'The Community', in James Q Wilson and Joan Petersilia (eds), *Crime* (San Francisco, Institute for Contemporary Studies, 1995), 193-194; towards the end of the nineteenth century, as Leon Radzinowicz has noted, Franz von Liszt, a founding father of the International Association of Criminal Law (IKV), 'had no doubts that in the final analysis a dynamic social policy would prove to be incomparably more potent than any criminal policy could ever be'. Sir Leon Radzinowicz, *The Roots of the International Association of Criminal Law and their Significance. A Tribute and a Re-assessment of the Centenary of the IKV.* (Freiburg, Max Planck Institute, 1991), 54. On the IKV, which was founded in 1889, Radzinowicz remarks that its proceedings were mostly concerned with criminal policy issues. He comments that IKV was 'a comfortable established élitist European club, earnestly engaged in thinking about and probing into the field of criminal justice at a time when Europe was at the height of its prestige and sophistication. And the main roads seemed to be leading towards progress.' (ibid., 9). This early development of criminal policy reflected the positivist enthusiasm

and social liberalism of the day. Consistent with the spirit of the times, Radzinowicz has commented elsewhere, it was widely believed that '(t)he study of crime and its control, in unison with all the other key disciplines relating to man in society,would ultimately provide explanations and solutions . . . It was only a question of time before the advance of civilization would effectively eradicate crime as a mass phenomenon.' Leon Radzinowicz, 'Penal Regressions', *Cambridge Law Journal,* 50 (1991), 423. This approach to criminal policy was born of optimism but it also carried with it the seeds which were to lead to a dark harvest with the rise in Germany of national socialism.

7. Heike Jung, 'Criminal Justice - A European Perspective', *Criminal Law Review* (April 1993), 238-239.

8. Auguste C 't Hart, 'Criminal Law Policy in The Netherlands' in Jan van Dijk, Charles Haffmans, Frits Rüter, Julian Schutte and Simon Stolwijk (eds), *Criminal Law in Action An overview of current issues in Western societies* (Deventer, Kluwer Law and Taxation Publishers, 1988), 73.

9. See for example, Maeve McMahon, 'Crime, Justice and Human Rights in the Baltics' (paper presented at the International Conference on Human Growth, Oslo, April, 1995); and Pawel Moczydlowski, 'Prison: From Communist System to Democracy. Transformation of the Polish Penitentiary System' (paper also presented at the Oslo Conference).

10. Paul Rock, 'Opening Stages of Criminal Justice Policy Making', *British Journal of Criminology*, 35 (1995), 16.

11. Andrew Ashworth, 'Principles, Practice and Criminal Justice', in Peter Birks (ed) *Pressing Problems in the Law, Volume 1, Criminal Justice and Human Rights* (Oxford, Oxford University Press, 1995), 43.

12. Nicola Lacey, 'Government as Manager, Citizen as Consumer: The Case of the Criminal Justice Act 1991' *Modern Law Review,* 57 (1994): 534-554.

13. Antonie A G Peters, 'Main Currents in Criminal Law Theory' in Jan van Dijk, Charles Haffmans, Frits Rüter, Julian Schutte and Simon Stolwijk (eds) *Criminal Law in Action An overview of current issues in Western societies* (Deventer, Kluwer Law and Taxation Publishers, 1988), 33.

14. Malcolm M Feeley, *Court Reform on Trial* (New York, Basic Books, 1983); a similar observation could be made with respect to sentencing reform in the United States; see for example, David F Greenberg and Drew Humphries, 'The Cooption of Fixed Sentencing Reform', *Crime and Delinquency,* 26 (1980): 210-225. In a recent exploration of the approach taken by the British Parliament and courts to serious fraud, A T H Smith has written: 'Rights are not treated by the British courts as imperatives, let alone as absolutes, but as expressions of value and policy, which may be compromised in pursuit of other social aims and policies. When the suppression of serious fraud is the objective, the experience is that the right counts for virtually nothing.' A T H Smith, 'The Right to Silence in Cases of Serious Fraud' in Peter Birks (ed) *Pressing Problems in the Law, Volume 1,*

Criminal Justice and Human Rights (Oxford, Oxford University Press, 1995), 81-88.

15. Leon Radzinowicz, 'Penal Regressions', *Cambridge Law Journal,* 50 (1991), 425.

16. ibid., 427.

17. René van Swaaningen and Gerard de Jonge, 'The Dutch Prison System and Penal Policy in the 1990s. From humanitarian paternalism to penal business management' in Mick Ryan and Vincenzo Ruggierro (eds),*Western European Penal Systems: A Critical Anatomy* (London, Sage, 1995). 24-45; see also Andrew Rutherford, *Criminal Justice and the Pursuit of Decency* (Winchester, Waterside Press, 1994); and Malcolm M Feeley and Jonathon Simon 'Actuarial Justice: the Emerging New Criminal Law' in David Nelkin (ed), *The Futures of Criminology,* (London, Sage, 1994), 173-201.

CHAPTER 2

Social Authoritarianism and Incapacitation

Crime was a peripheral issue in the presidential election of 1964, but it did have one notable consequence. Senator Barry Goldwater's 'crime in the streets' rhetoric prompted the decision by President Lyndon Johnson in July 1965 to set up his Commission on Law Enforcement and the Administration of Justice, under the chairmanship of the Attorney General, Nicholas Katzenbach. When the Crime Commission's report, *The Challenge of Crime in a Free Society* was published in February 1967, it was apparent immediately that the commission members had held largely to the liberal optimism inherent in President Johnson's notion of a Great Society. The report declared:

> In the last analysis, the most promising and so the most important method of dealing with crime is preventing it - by ameliorating the conditions of life that drive people to commit crimes and that undermine the restraining rules and institutions erected by society against anti-social conduct. That sense of stake, of something that can be gained or lost, can come only through real opportunity for full participation in society's life and growth. It is insuring opportunity that is the basic goal of prevention programs[1]

The agencies of criminal justice had the crucial but necessarily narrow role of responding effectively and fairly to the more serious offenders. Virtually all of the official responses to crime would continue to be at the local and state levels of government, but the various federal authorities were urged to make 'a dramatic new contribution to the national effort against crime' by greatly expanding the support they were able to offer.

The publication of the Crime Commission's report and the subsequent Omnibus Crime Control and Safe Streets Act of 1968 (the main aspect of which was to establish the Law Enforcement Assistance Administration) coincided with a hardening political climate. Indeed, in the judgement of one public opinion survey analyst, over the twenty year period from the mid-1960s the growth in public support for a tougher stance on offenders and crime was 'one of the few issues (where) we can document a clear, substantial shift to the right.'[2] A further indicator of the mood and temper of the times was the state prison population, which had declined by 14% between 1962-68 , but then rose by 4% between 1969-72 and by 74% between 1973-78.[3] By the end of the 1970s the tide had completely turned, and the combined state and federal prison population more than trebled over the next decade. Within less than a generation, virtually all traces of the Crime Commission's vision of criminal policy had vanished. The metamorphosis can be understood, at least in part, in terms of 'the collapse of the liberal faith in the capacity of man to compel the world, both natural and social, to provide an endless series of benefits.'[4] Within the United States, this collapse was given particular poignancy by the extraordinary and traumatic events of the 1960s which, as Daniel Moynihan observed, began with the promise of a golden age but ended in nightmare.[5]

The criminal policy agenda which emerged for the 1970s and beyond was shaped less by President Johnson's Crime Commission than by a largely different set of assumptions and concerns. A key player throughout this period of transformation was a member of the Crime Commission's huge cast of academic advisors, James Q Wilson.[6] In his advisory role Wilson had an early opportunity to reflect on the relationship between criminological expertise and the policy-making process. He subsequently recalled that

> few social scientists made careful distinctions, when the chips were down, between what they knew as scholars and what they believed as citizens, or even spent much time discussing the complex relationships between knowledge and belief. I certainly did not, and I do not recall others doing so.[7]

Referring to his Harvard colleague, Lloyd Ohlin, who had served as one of the associate directors of the Crime Commission, Wilson recalled: 'It was only gradually, as I became involved in various advisory roles, that I realized that what is interesting is not necessarily useful. In short, I did not, any more than Professor Ohlin, have in 1966-68 empirically supported policy advice to offer statesmen dealing with crime.'[8] Lloyd Ohlin, whose own research on urban delinquency had made a considerable impact on the design of the Mobilization for Youth Program in the early 1960s and later upon the perspective developed by the Crime Commission,[9] had acknowledged that the Commission was influenced by existing 'social science concepts, theories and general perspectives' and that these had cast grave doubts on the effectiveness of criminal justice and had given rise to such notions as deprisonisation and criminal justice as a last resort. Wilson was particularly impressed by Ohlin's comment that the staff had successfully persuaded a conservative commission to accept 'far more liberal recommendations . . . than one would have thought possible at the outset.'[10] Perhaps with Ohlin in mind, Wilson cryptically observed:

> When those who practice it (sociology) are brought forward and asked for advice, they will say either (if conservative) that nothing is possible, or (if liberal) that everything is possible. That most sociologists are liberals explains why the latter reaction is more common, even though the presumptions of their own discipline would more naturally lead to the former.[11]

Wilson's personal experience and reflections upon the work of the Crime Commission provided him with a reference point to which he regularly returned.[12]

James Q Wilson majored in political science at the University of Redlands, on the outskirts of San Bernardino in southern California. After three years as a naval officer he enrolled at the University of Chicago to undertake research on city governance under Edward C Banfield. His doctoral dissertation on the involvement of blacks in Chicago city politics was published in 1960, and three years later he and Banfield co-authored *City Politics*.[13] In 1961 he moved to the department of government at Harvard where he was to remain for the next twenty-six years. As Wilson later put it, he had entered 'criminology through the backdoor'[14] as a result of undertaking a comparative study of policing within its local political context, which involved 'hundreds of hours in patrol cars'.[15] While he continued to address policing issues from time to time, his interest in crime soon enjoyed a much wider span.[16] Wilson returned to California in 1987 to take up the James A Collins Chair of Management and Public Policy at the University of California, Los Angeles. By the early 1990s he had moved onto the yet wider stage of human character,[17] and to some degree his mantle on crime issues had been passed to a former student and close academic associate, John J DiIulio.[18]

It was at Harvard, where he occupied the Henry Lee Shattuck Chair of Government from 1973-1987, that Wilson's influence on criminal policy issues was at its peak. He was a natural counterpoint to Lloyd Ohlin who became the professor of criminology at Harvard Law School in 1967. But as the 1970s unfolded it was Wilson and not Ohlin who was most in step with the spirit of the times. DiIulio, for example, entertained no doubts as to his stature, in a tribute written in 1991 when Wilson became president of the American Political Science Association.

It is one measure of his boundless energy and creativity that he accelerated his career as one of the nation's leading criminal justice analysts while continuing his career as one of its most insightful political analysts.[19]

Wilson's national stature as a political scientist, based upon several leading texts on government, political organizations and comparative bureaucracies lent credibility to his equally prodigious output on crime.[20] As Wilson, himself, put it: 'I was not in 1966 a criminologist, nor am I now. I came to crime, if I may put it that way, as a consequence of my study of police administration and its political context, and found myself labelled an ''expert'' on crime because of that interest.'[21] In a mordant retort, Benedict Alper wrote: 'Finding himself taken seriously by those who employed his services, he is apparently persuaded to take himself seriously as well. From this point on, he does not hesitate to pontificate on matters which until now have been neither the subject of his concern nor his scholarship.'[22]

WILSON'S WAY OF THINKING ABOUT CRIMINAL POLICY

With the publication of *Thinking About Crime* in 1975, James Q Wilson became America's best known commentator on criminal policy. His no nonsense message became an instant landmark largely because it so deftly caught the hardening political mood.[23] The reshaping of the American discourse on criminal policy was already well underway by the early 1970s, but it was given sharper definition by the publication of *Thinking About Crime*. Wilson's elegant prose, sardonic wit and sharp turn of phrase connected these public policy issues to an unusually wide readership. In DiIulio's view, the book

> single-handedly revolutionised the contemporary study of crime by showing how the best empirical data then available supported, or at least did nothing to undercut, the common sense and rudimentary micro-economics of the subject; namely that if crime pays, more crimes will be committed but if the real or perceived penalties for crime are swift, certain and severe, fewer crimes will be committed.[24]

Although reworked and updated, most of the book had already been published in articles or essays, the first of which had appeared in 1968. The concluding chapter which contained new material on

22

incapacitation was reprinted as a newspaper article, 'Lock 'Em Up and Other Thoughts about Crime'. [25]

The significance of *Thinking About Crime* was roundly acknowledged and, thereafter, much discussion of criminal policy in the United States, and often further afield, has taken account of Wilson's writings.[26] For example, a leading commentator, Charles E Silberman, after remarking that 'few scholars have had so profound an influence on contemporary thought about crime,' located Wilson within a long tradition of distinguishing between the 'deserving' and 'undeserving' poor.[27] In Britain, Paul Rock astutely recognized that the book was 'not just another poring over the familiar imponderables of an insulated discipline. And it might well become a political fact whose effects merit monitoring.' Although Rock regarded Wilson as

> the criminologically marginal man whose thought possesses all the illumination and deformation of an eccentric perspective . . . (his) restoration of a common-sense context for criminology is doubly important: not only does it depart from scholastic orthodoxy by lodging argument in an environment of practical concerns, it also develops an analysis which might actually have significant political consequences.[28]

And for Jerome Skolnick of the University of California, there was little doubt as to the ultimate sinister destination of Wilson's ideas. After remarking upon his 'characteristic combination of literary flair and scant evidence', he concluded that, 'either we attend to altering the social and economic bases of crime or we grope our way towards a false realism - a garrison state, increasingly controlled by those possessing the force of arms and the keys to the prison.'[29]

By the end of the 1970s Wilson's already prolific writings amounted to a distinctive contribution to the criminal policy agenda of federal and state governments intent on being seen to take action. For Wilson, the essential basis of any policy discussion was 'a proper understanding of man and the publicly controllable forces to which he will respond, coupled with only moderate expectations about what can be accomplished under even the best of circumstances . . .'[30] Ordinary people were anxious about street crime, and it was to their concerns that he directly addressed himself. His wholehearted endorsement of imprisonment provided a graphic contrast to the de-escalatory language of the Crime Commission.[31] Reduced to its essence, Wilson's vision of criminal policy rested upon the presumption that the problem facing America was one of street criminals who could be identified and set apart from respectable people. In the case of serious and repetitive offenders, society should be protected through a more

23

vigorous use of the prison system; less serious offenders needed to be excluded from decent society through short spells in prison or in other ways. The connecting policy theme was that of exclusion: a 'we-they' divide that remained at the heart of his writings on criminal policy over a thirty year period. It was a theme which made a particularly strong impact in the United States during the 1980s.

Wilson's central proposition was that statesmen and citizens had shared a false assumption that no problem is addressed until its causes are eliminated. He unequivocally rejected the Crime Commission's leitmotif that the underlying causes of crime had to be tackled. He declared, in a phrase with which he will always be associated, that he had 'yet to see a "root cause", or to encounter a government program that has successfully attacked it.' Searching for causal solutions was dismissed as 'a way of deferring any action and criticizing any policy'.[32] He contended that the difficulty arose from 'confusing causal analysis with policy analysis'.[33] His reading of two leading criminological texts, Sutherland and Cressey's *Principles of Criminology* and Cloward and Ohlin's *Delinquency and Opportunity*, was that neither had been able to provide a plausible basis for public policy in achieving 'a reduction in specified forms of crime'.[34] Policy analysis, as opposed to causal analysis, began with a very different perspective, leading Wilson to conclude that

the criminologist, concerned with causal explanations and part of a discipline - sociology - that assumes that social processes determine behaviour, has operated largely within an intellectual framework that makes it difficult or impossible to develop reasonable policy alternatives and has cast doubt, by assumption more than by argument or evidence, on the efficacy of those policy tools, necessarily dealing with objective rather than subjective conditions, which society might use to alter crime rates. A serious policy-oriented analysis of crime would, by contrast, place heavy emphasis on manipulation of objective conditions, not necessarily because of a belief that the "causes of crime" are thereby being eradicated, but because behaviour is easier to change than attitudes, and because the only instruments society has by which to alter behaviour in the short run require it to assume that people act in response to the costs and benefits of alternative courses of action.[35]

As a political scientist, Wilson frequently was impressed with the accordance of conclusions drawn from his assessment of the evidence on crime and offenders and the common sense views of ordinary people. In fashioning a basis for criminal policy, he saw his mission as one of closing the gap between élite and popular opinion. He was in no doubt as to whose ground had to be conceded. As he wrote two years after the appearance of *Thinking About Crime*, '(s)ince our current crime wave began in about 1963, popular opinion has been receptive to policies that élite and intellectual opinion is only now coming to accept. The signs of policy change that we can detect seem to be caused by what the few now think rather that what the many long believed.'[36] This statement represents the crux of Wilson's approach to criminal policy and does much to explain the extent and depth of his influence. The rousing conclusion to *Thinking About Crime* can be viewed as a direct appeal to populist political opinion:

> Intellectuals, although they often dislike the common person as an individual, do not wish to be caught saying uncomplimentary things about humankind. Nevertheless, some people will shun crime even if we do nothing to deter them, while others will seek it out even if we do everything to reform them. Wicked people exist. Nothing avails except to set them apart from innocent people. And many people, neither wicked nor innocent, but watchful, dissembling, and calculating of their opportunities, ponder our reactions to wickedness as a cue to what they might profitably do. We have trifled with the wicked, made sport of the innocent, and encouraged the calculators. Justice suffers, and so do we all.[37]

Wilson drew attention to the extent to which the liberal viewpoint on the crime issue had moved in a conservative direction. Commenting upon this emerging confluence in a 1971 article, 'Crime and the Liberal Audience', he contended that during the 1960s liberals had abdicated the crime issue to the political right.[38] However, by 1970 'enough members of the liberal audience had had their typewriters stolen to make it difficult to write articles denying the existence of a crime wave.'[39] A few years later, he was persuaded that intellectual and liberal resistance to thinking about crime and taking seriously the punitive aspects of criminal justice had been lessened, although political action was still lacking.[40] By 1983, however, he contended that the main difference between conservatives and liberals on crime turned on the manipulation of the costs of crime or the benefits of non-crime. Whereas the older debate about crime involved very different assumptions about human nature: that it was fundamentally good or bad, liberals and conservatives now embraced the same theory of human nature and the existing choices amounted to little more than a 'policy quibble'.[41]

In *Thinking About Crime* Wilson argued 'for a sober view of man and his institutions that would permit reasonable things to be accomplished, foolish things abandoned, and utopian things forgotten. A sober view of man requires a modest definition of progress.'[42] He was, he insisted, the calm social scientist, who was able to stand aside from the political hurly burley. Writing in 1975, he observed:

> In the next ten years, I hope that we can learn to experiment rather than to simply spend, to test our theories rather than fund our fears. This is advice, not simply or even primarily to government - for governments are run by men and women who are under irresistible pressures to pretend that they know more than they do - but to my colleagues: academics, theoreticians, writers, advisers.[43]

Following a critical appraisal of the revised edition of *Thinking About Crime*, in which Elliott Currie had described him as a leading representative of the conservative position on crime, Wilson retorted that when he published the first edition he had 'wanted among other things, to persuade readers that *both* the liberal *and* the conservative positions of the time were in error'. With Ramsey Clark and Richard Nixon in his mind as exemplars of these respective positions, he declared both to be wrong.[44] The conservative position had been the easier one to rebut. There was fragmentary evidence that specialized police squads targeting high-rate offenders might make a difference, but there was little evidence that the severity of penalties (as opposed to their certainty) had an effect on crime rates. Nor did research support the conservative assumption that there was a technological quick fix for crime. For Wilson, the liberal position was more difficult to deal with, being based less on faith in technology than upon what he regarded as a false view of human nature. Liberals viewed man as being the product of his environment and held that by making marginal alterations to that environment, one could alter human behaviour in predictable and desirable ways. Wilson did not believe there was any evidence to support such a view; furthermore, he was worried that the agenda of some liberals was not to reduce crime but to remake society.

> What I did oppose were untested hopes, and the ideology that sustained them: with social policies as with police tactics, I wanted experiments conducted that would find out what works. I'm certain Mr Currie views me as an ideologue, loving to punish and hating to help, but he is wrong; I am, or try to be, a pragmatist.[45]

Wilson accepted the value of some interventions, particularly within schools, but in the meantime, 'justice alone, to say nothing of a

26

desire to reduce crime, requires that the guilty be punished. Wicked people *do* exist, and a just society cannot treat them with the leniency advocated by the dwindling but still ardent band of prison opponents.'[46] In a robust rejoinder, Currie maintained that far from simply being a pragmatist, Wilson had to be viewed as:

> an ardent and influential advocate of a view of crime that rests on certain important political assumptions - particularly the common conservative insistence on the limits of government . . . Wilson's writings have in fact been among the most important intellectual underpinnings of an approach to crime that has stressed incarceration at the expense of more constructive preventive social action. That choice is not pragmatic, but political.[47]

Few observers would regard as contentious a recent assessment of James Q Wilson as being 'for two decades the country's leading conservative scholar of crime control policy and research.'[48]

Wilson was always astutely aware of the roles open to academics within the spheres of public policy-making. Looking back to the mid-1960s, he wrote that

> intellectuals framed, and to a large degree conducted, the debates about whether this language and these paradigms were correct. The most influential intellectuals were those who managed to link a concept or a theory to the practical needs and ideological predispositions of political activists and government officials.[49]

He noted that in the 1960s intellectuals were asked for their advice and their findings and gave copiously of the former and sparingly of the latter. Rarely, however, did they actually devise a programme or initiate a policy. 'Contrary to what their critics often suppose, intellectuals are not usually the authors of particular policies.'[50] Wilson was not suggesting that these intellectuals were without influence; quite the contrary. But they were influential not in the realm of detailed policy guidance but in terms of 'the conceptual language, the ruling paradigms, the empirical examples (note that I say examples, not evidence) that became the accepted assumptions for those in charge of making policy.'[51] In 1981, when Wilson wrote this article, he had already established a position of unrivalled academic influence which he was to retain throughout the Reagan and Bush years. He cannot have had any misconception that his vision of criminal policy was in tune with the 'ideological predispositions' of the government of the day.

A departmental colleague at Harvard may have had Wilson in mind when he observed:

Reaganism grows from a bond forged between different groups that previously had little to do with each other . . . Ronald Reagan's coalition also makes alliances with the neoconservatives, those disgruntled New Deal Democrats whose intellects crowd the pages of journals such as *The Public Interest* and *Commentary*. For the neoconservatives, Reaganism corrects the liberal permissiveness of the 1960s and 1970s, reintroduces the Republican virtues of decentralization, and stands tough-minded on law, order and national security.[52]

Furthermore, the advocates of Reaganism 'know what kind of society they want and America needs. By contrast, progressive liberalism is usually defensive and vague with regard to purpose.'[53] Liberals were challenged as to what they could propose to address people's concerns about crime. Wilson was successful, in part, precisely because he had clear and firm proposals. While it was unclear as to just what liberals were proposing, Wilson had an agenda that people could understand and support. From its outset, Reaganism also represented a counter-culture and the high ground had to be secured before addressing its ambitious agenda. Revealingly, Wilson compared the mood at the start of the 1980s with the era of two decades earlier:

In the sixties, the ideas in question were those of liberal intellectuals and, since liberalism had long been the governing ideology of American politics, the intellectuals then in vogue were brimming with the kind of self-confidence that comes from the belief that they were in the vanguard of an irreversible historical impulse. Today, the ideas that seem to influence the administration of President Reagan are about how best to reverse, or at least stem, a political tide that has been running for half a century or more. Not surprisingly, these ideas are more controversial and their proponents feel more embattled than did their predecessors of two decades ago. In the 1960s, the policy "intellectuals" saw themselves as priests of the established order; today, their counterparts think of themselves as missionaries in a hostile country.[54]

Wilson has always been determined to go beyond the armchair in thinking and writing about criminal policy. From early in his academic career, he has been actively engaged in a variety of advisory and consultative roles as well as serving on commissions and task forces. For example, he served as a panel member on successive panels set up by the National Academy of Sciences which, since the late 1970s, have scrutinized selected areas of criminal policy research. In 1981, Wilson suggested that 'the role intellectuals as scholars (rather than as partisan advocates or insightful citizens) can play in the making of public policy is likely to be small.'[55] This reflection, however, did not deter him from serving on two official task forces during that year: on youth crime for the governor of Massachusetts and for the Reagan administration on violent crime.[56]

Wilson justifies his almost exclusive interest in 'street crime' on the grounds that this is what concerns most people. He has little to say about such matters as fraud or violence within the home. Nor has he displayed interest in crime causation except in terms of individuals calculating what they regard to be in their best interests. However, in the mid-1980s, together with Richard J Herrnstein, a Harvard psychologist, he did turn his attention to constitutional factors, early family influences and social circumstances. But, *Crime and Human Nature: The definitive study of the causes of crime*, despite its subtitle, did not represent a significant departure from Wilson's underlying policy prescription that the wicked and the good can and should be separated.[57] This policy presumption has remained paramount in his approach to imprisonment, illegal drugs and crime prevention.

FEELING GOOD ABOUT PRISON

James Q Wilson's most distinctive contribution has been to articulate a non-apologetic endorsement of imprisonment as the core component of criminal policy. The role of prisons had been the subject of much debate during the 1960s and into the early 1970s, with the widely held view that too many people were imprisoned; that prisons were violent and damaging places contributing to the crime problem; and that the over-representation of blacks among the prison population reflected gross discrimination if not a racist political agenda. The decline in prison numbers during the 1960s reflected this pervasive unease about the use of imprisonment within a civilised process of justice. The Crime Commission was only one of several official voices encouraging the search by the courts for effective community-based sentences. The tragic events in upper New York State at Attica prison in 1971, during which forty-one people were killed, cast a further shadow across American prisons. Along with others, Wilson challenged this gloomy view of prison by endorsing a politics of good conscience about the use of imprisonment. He did not simply defend the status quo and argue against deinstitutionalization, but he was unequivocal in calling for the expansion of the federal and state prison systems. Wilson's task in this respect was made all the easier because by the 1970s liberal reformers were concerned primarily with attempting to construct punishment procedures which relied upon fairness and certainty, leaving the prison ideology largely intact within any new sentencing structure.[58]

More than any other single person, Wilson popularized deterrence and incapacitation as the twin functions neatly provided by the prison. He bestowed an academic respectability upon these concepts within the public policy arena, even though they remained unresolved on either effectiveness or ethical grounds. His sustained belief in deterrence as an instrument of penal policy reflects a view of people as calculating their opportunities, and he was convinced by his reading of the research literature that '(t)he deterrent capacity of criminal penalties is supported by statistical data for large numbers of offenses over long periods of time.' [59] Three years later, however, a research panel of the National Academy of Sciences reported that it had failed to locate any evidence that supported the effectiveness of deterrence strategies.[60] Despite his membership of the panel, Wilson continued to insist that it was premature to write off deterrence, maintaining that 'it is difficult, but not impossible, to achieve increased deterrent effects through changes in the law.'[61] But by now an element of caution was apparent, with Wilson arguing that

> the wisest course of action for society is to try simultaneously to increase both the benefits of non-crime and the costs of crime, all the while bearing in mind that no feasible changes in either part of the equation is likely to produce big changes in crime rates.[62]

As support for the deterrence strategy faded within the research community, Wilson's enthusiasm for incapacitation seemed to know no bounds. As Wilson saw it, there was 'one great advantage to incapacitation as a crime control strategy - namely, it does not require us to make any assumptions about human nature.'[63] In the first instance, he had been impressed by the notion of 'chronic offenders' which emerged from the longitudinal study by Marvin Wolfgang and colleagues at the University of Pennsylvania. Six percent of the ten thousand boys in the cohort were found to be responsible for more than half the recorded offences committed by the group as a whole.[64] Although Wolfgang had concluded that 'the juvenile justice system, at its best, has no effect on the subsequent behaviour of adolescent boys and, at its worst, has a deleterious effect on future behaviour'[65], this was not the conclusion that Wilson took from the study, but rather the thought that the 'chronic' offenders could be identified and isolated.

30

At about the same time Wilson was greatly encouraged to learn of on-going work to construct mathematically an incapacitation model, undertaken by Benjamin Avi-Itzhak and Reuel Shinnar of the School of Engineering at the City College of New York and Shlomo Shinnar of the Albert Einstein College of Medicine. Wilson drew heavily from a still unpublished study by the Shinnars who, on the basis of New York crime data and some major assumptions where data were missing (most notably regarding patterns of offending), claimed 'that a policy of uniform prison sentences for convicted criminals could under present conditions reduce *safety* crime by a factor of four to five . . . We are convinced that with reasonable, carefully designed policies, the crime rate could be significantly reduced in a short time.'[66] Although Wilson acknowledged that the Shinnars' estimates were based on 'uncertain data and involve assumptions that can be challenged' he was confident that 'even assuming they are overly optimistic by a factor or two, a sizeable reduction in crime would still ensue.'[67]

Wilson's gloss on the Shinnars' study together with his strident endorsement of incapacitation as an instrument of effective criminal policy made a powerful impact. Indeed, it was in large part the claims that Wilson made for both deterrence and incapacitation that prompted the National Academy of Sciences to establish its panel on deterrent and incapacitative effects. The caution expressed by the panel, when it reported in 1978 regarding claims made for deterrence, has already been mentioned. With respect to incapacitation the panel drew attention to a host of technical, ethical and legal problems

of explicitly imprisoning people to avoid crimes they commit in the future . . . Poor prediction not only undermines the utilitarian justification for selectively incapacitating some convicted offenders, but it also introduces concern for the injustice suffered by those who are imprisoned because their future crime propensity is erroneously predicted to be higher than it is.[68]

But Wilson's popularisation of deterrence and incapacitation went far beyond the policy research community, and his enthusiasm for imprisonment was regularly cited. For example, President Gerald Ford has recalled that four months after becoming President,

I had a chance to talk with Harvard Professor James Q Wilson. After our conversation, he sent me a copy of his book *Thinking About Crime*, which I read with great interest. One of his major points was that most serious crimes were committed by repeat offenders, people who had been convicted before. Another was that too many Americans had forgotten that the primary purpose of imprisonment was *not* to rehabilitate the convicted criminal so that he could return to society, but to punish him and keep him off the streets. The *certainty* of having to spend a specified time behind bars after being convicted of a serious offense, Wilson maintained, was more important as a deterrent than almost anything else. Finally, Wilson worried that the nation's opinion formers were focusing their concerns on the criminal and not on the victims of criminal acts. His points made a lot of sense to me . . . I decided to use his arguments for the detailed proposals that I would submit to Congress . . .[69]

The brief life of the Ford administration did not permit action to be taken on these legislative proposals, although in 1975 the Law Enforcement Administration Agency created and funded 'career criminal' prosecution programmes.[70]

The significance of what Wilson had to say about incapacitation and chronic offenders had less to do with specific statutes or programmes than with the encouragement it gave to a burgeoning punitive culture. Wilson's most direct opportunity to carry forward his idea of the prison as an effective instrument of crime reduction arose from his appointment by the Reagan Administration to an eight member Task Force on Violent Crime, with a mandate of only one hundred and twenty days to complete its report.[71] The task force agreed immediately upon a wide definition of violent crime that embraced all 'serious crime' and which, in addition to violence, included 'those other serious offenses - such as arson, drug trafficking, weapons offenses, and household burglaries - that may or may not lead to injury.'[72] Wilson wrote the report's opening section which narrowly restricted the scope for action by the federal government.[73] With the abolition of LEEA in 1981, many observers were concerned that the federal government was finally abandoning the leadership role which had been charted for it by the Crime Commission. But Wilson's influence extended beyond issues of new federalism, and there can be little doubt that he left his mark on the tone and substance of the report. In the introduction, for example, readers were informed that: 'The wave of serious, violent crime we are now experiencing reflects a breakdown of the social order, not of the legal order'; and that: 'Citizens will never understand the failure of the criminal justice system to excuse the innocent and punish the guilty . . . The citizen wants safety and expects justice; too often, he or she gets neither.'[74]

Many of the report's specific recommendations reflected Wilson's preoccupations of the previous decade, not least those which dealt with research and the development of federal and state programmes addressed to 'career criminals'. The task force followed Wilson's lead

32

in urging the need for an integrated view of offending that overcame the traditional barrier between juvenile justice and the adult criminal justice process. One outcome was to challenge some of the traditional protections afforded to juveniles, in particular, to enable prosecutors to use a juvenile's offending record as a predictor; and to amend the law so as to allow the fingerprinting of all juveniles convicted of serious offenses in federal courts. Three years earlier Wilson and a colleague had argued that a separate juvenile justice system interfered with the need to assemble information on which practitioners could act with regard to intensive offenders.

> To identify intensive offenders as early as possible, it will be necessary to photograph and fingerprint juveniles who commit serious crimes, especially violent ones; to allow them to be identified in line-ups; and to compile such information so that any criminal justice agency (but not persons outside it) would have a complete record on intensive or violent offenders available at all points in the process, and in the nearby jurisdictions.[75]

The task force also recommended that the Bail Reform Act of 1966 be amended, so as to permit dangerousness to be taken into account in pretrial release decision-making.[76] Furthermore, the task force maintained without qualification that a direct and simple relationship existed between violent crime and imprisonment. Noting that the number of state prisoners had increased by twenty-three percent between 1978-1981, the report observed: 'The overriding concern remains the safety of the community which is secured by ensuring that those offenders, i.e. serious, violent offenders, who need to be incapacitated are incarcerated.'[77] The recommendation of a $2 billion federal appropriation over four years to support prison construction at the state level was described by the governor of Illinois, James R Thompson, co-chairman of the task force, as being the 'linchpin' for all the other recommendations, with the 'bottom line' being that, 'we have to lock up more violent offenders and we have to keep them locked up.'[78] In terms of method, resources and substance the task force was 'swift in its construction and modest in its innovative capacities',[79] and a very poor cousin of its various predecessors since the Wickersham Commission in the 1920s. The report, however, did contribute to the policies, practices and public mood which prompted the quantum leap in the nation's prison population over the next decade.

The Reagan administration was especially receptive to the task force's recommendation that the Justice Department conduct research

33

on operationalising the concept of 'career criminals'. By this time, policy researchers were convinced that the way forward lay in the improvement of estimates of the individual offender's rates of offending over specified periods of time. If repeat offenders could be so identified, generalized notions of incapacitation might then give way to selective incapacitation. Attention was once again focused on where Wilson's interest had started - upon 'chronic' or 'career' offenders. As two leading researchers observed,

> the idea of the career criminal does not in itself suggest complexity or difficulty. On the contrary, it suggests simple, clear-thinking policy directed at the heart of the crime problem . . . To the policy-oriented, the idea of a career criminal suggests the possibility of doing something to or for a small segment of the criminal population with notable reductions in crime rates.[80]

Noting the circularity of policy research on career criminals, they remarked that 'discovery of the career criminal by criminologists stimulated the idea of selective incapacitation. To implement the idea of selective incapacitation, one need only identify career criminals. Unfortunately, the career criminals who suggested the idea in the first place cannot be found when it comes to implement the policy.' It turns out that they are no longer active. 'When asked to identify career criminals in advance of their criminal careers, the research community requests additional funding.'[81] The researchers concluded that federal research policy, having been captured by the 'career criminal' notion, presupposed 'considerable confidence in the validity of the ideas being pursued, and considerable lack of confidence in alternative perspectives.'[82]

Within three or four years some results of this huge investment of research funding began to surface, and once again Wilson was to play a key role. Of the various federal research projects, the largest had been awarded to the RAND Corporation, based in Santa Monica, California. It was one of the RAND studies which seemed to Wilson to offer a dramatic way forward. On the basis of interviews in which prisoners were asked about their criminal activities, Peter Greenwood and Allan Abrahamse made separate estimates of offence rates for low, medium and high rate offenders, calculating the assumed crime reduction effects of imprisoning persons for different periods for each of these groups. By this method, Greenwood and Abrahamse suggested that by imposing longer prison sentences on high-rate offenders the robbery rate could be reduced by up to twenty percent, without significantly increasing the prison population.[83] These findings

...ade for the incapacitation model had to be scaled down. In a paper prepared for the panel, Christy A Visher stated: "On the basis of this ...analysis, much more realistic estimates of the true operation of ...ffectiveness of a prediction instrument are needed before the current enthusiasm about the estimated reduction in crime through selective incapacitation is warranted."[] Another consultant to the panel, Mark Moore, warned of the technocratic enthusiasm for prediction.[] The following year, Peter Greenwood himself, was urging that his scale be treated with caution since its predictive accuracy did not appear to justify the large differences in sentence length for offenders in different categories that would be necessary to achieve significant selective incapacitative effects...[]

Despite these attacks, Wilson remained an unwavering advocate of incapacitation. As Andrew von Hirsch has remarked, with faint surprise:

> ...puzzling only is the emotional quality of the response in Wilson's ...statement of Greenwood's selective incapacitation. Albeit harshly utilitarian ...disappointed ... in his strategies, they are reserved enthusiasm ...to advocacy of selective incapacitation truly, it would seem of hope ...there pursues.[]

Wilson, in return, has been equally dismissive of the opponents of incapacitation, claiming they are not essentially interested in the ...violence reduction, but get all worked up about their underlying ...liberal claim against...

> ...much of the debate about incapacitation is not about its crime reduction ...potential, but rather the connection between imprisonment and social concern for ...appropriate conditions. Liberals set out a set of diversionary arguments ...designed to make imprisonment penalty, they look as bad as possible while ...side stepping incarceration as much as with the best of their choices."[]

A decade or so later he maintained that his vision of criminal policy did not conflict with the values of a free society, concluding that "(s)ome people think larger prison population is inconsistent with freedom or a sign that a society deserves one like that god... they... They are quite wrong. Every... is now discovering this sobering truth as we are..."

"...we as the observers of the American criminal policy scene have described, liberals by sinuous path of the notion of incapacitation, begins with dramatic initial claims, is followed by modification, and ends in chilly realism tempered by the hope that future research may uncover some opportunities for improvement in current practice.'[94] There are indeed striking parallels between the pattern of events around the publication of the first and the revised editions of *Thinking About Crime*. In both instances Wilson championed barely completed research. In the late 1970s the notion of general incapacitation did not withstand close academic scrutiny. Much the same fate awaited selective incapacitation in the mid-1980s. However, it was Wilson's endorsement of incapacitation throughout this period that made the most impact on public policy and not the cautious conclusions of the research panellists and other academics. Wilson's championship of deterrence and incapacitation had less impact on specific sentencing reforms than it did in terms of reviving a generalized enthusiasm for the prison. To a large extent, the impact was at the level of practice, with an expanding pro-custody ethos guiding the decisions of practitioners across the criminal justice process. Prison populations escalated in most states, regardless of whether or not far-reaching revisions of sentencing statutes had occurred.[95] While state legislatures did not enact provisions that directly drew from ideas about selective incapacitation, they were more than receptive to proposals for mandatory terms of imprisonment for specified offences.[96] Andrew von Hirsch observed that 'in the flurry of legislative activity on sentencing during this era, Wilson's views and those of his colleagues were influential and frequently cited.'[97]

In the fifteen years between 1975, when *Thinking About Crime* was published, and 1990 the federal and state prison populations rose from 240,593 to 774,375, an increase of 221 percent.[98] To a considerable extent, much of this extraordinary escalation in prison numbers was driven by the hardening attitudes of practitioners, among whom Wilson had played no small part in restoring 'the good name of prisons'.[99] Wilson certainly had practitioners as much as policy-makers in mind in his writings, and was quite specific on this point in an edited volume of essays published in 1983, when he suggested that

> the most effective (in terms of crime reduction) career criminal programs would be those that routinely examine the juvenile as well as the adult arrest record of arrestees, that routinely conduct urinalysis of arrestees in order to identify drug users, and that worry more about young adults who are at or near the peak of their criminal activity . . .

He was concerned that breaches of probation were not being taken seriously by busy and harassed officials, which sent the message that such transgressions were costless and worth repeating. 'This is especially the case when the transgression represents a violation of an explicit contract with society.'[100]

WARS ON DRUGS

In 1990 Wilson, together with Michael Tonry, edited *Drugs and Crime* in the Crime and Justice series for the University of Chicago. In the concluding chapter, Wilson wrote:

> I have watched several "wars on drugs" declared over the last three decades. The wars typically begin with a statement that the time for studies is past and the time for action has come. "We know what to do; let's get on with it." In fact, we do not know what to do in any comprehensive way, and the need for research is never more urgent than at the beginning of a "war". That is because every past war has led, after brief gains, to final defeat. And so we condemn another generation to risk.[101]

While portraying himself as providing a rational and research led middle course, Wilson has never wavered from the view that the criminal law should play a tough role, sometimes alongside medical programmes. Confronting illegal drugs has been a key aspect of his approach to criminal policy which has remained broadly in step with the escalatory use of imprisonment for drug offenders. Wilson supported law enforcement efforts to reduce demand by going after the user, but had seemingly nothing to say about the increasingly severe sentencing of drugs offenders. He certainly cannot be counted among those who attempted to restrain the excesses of the anti-drug policies of the 1980s.

During the two decades preceding 1980, federal policy on illegal drugs reflected, with slight variations in emphasis, the themes of repression, treatment and prevention. While the Kennedy administration had promised an enhanced medical perspective, the Johnson and Nixon presidencies sought to balance these main themes reflecting, in the phrase of one close observer, 'the split-personality modern era in American drug policy'.[102] Between 1972-3 Wilson chaired the National Advisory Council on Drug Abuse Prevention, and it was during this period that he first addressed the increased use of heroin.[103] The bottom line for Wilson was clear: the state had some responsibility for the quality of life, and for a sufficiently large number of persons, heroin is so destructive that it should not be made generally available. He advocated going after the user; heroin should

38

be made scarce and at a high price to prevent the recruitment of new addicts (which must take precedence over improving the lives of confirmed users). Within the context of strong law enforcement, Wilson supported maintenance programmes for heroin addicts, characteristically noting that these did not attempt to address the 'root causes' of addiction. He was doubtful, however, that much would be achieved if these programmes were only available on a voluntary basis, concluding that 'a substantial measure of legal compulsion will have to accompany any treatment program.'[104]

In his assessment of federal drugs policy in the mid-1970s, Charles E Silberman noted that Wilson was hailing the Nixon anti-drug program as a model of successful law enforcement. Silberman caustically commented that as a consultant to federal agencies concerned with law enforcement and heroin use, Wilson had helped devise the policies he found so successful.[105] In 'The Sick Sixties', an article written for *The Atlantic Monthly* with Dr Robert Dupont (who later became director of the National Institute on Drug Abuse), Wilson explored the increased heroin addiction in Washington DC, in part attributing the heroin 'epidemic' in that city to the media's celebration of the youth culture and the cult of personal liberation.[106] Wilson also surmised that 'social programs designed to combat poverty brought together groups that once would have been isolated from each other, and thus spread the contagion as surely as bringing men together in the Army during World War One spread the influenza epidemic.'[107]

The pace of the wars on drugs was stepped up considerably during the Reagan and Bush presidencies. As Arnold Trebach has noted, when President Reagan took office in 1981, he was determined that this was a war he would actually win. While much of the focus was on hard drugs, a major target was marijuana which Dr Robert Dupont described as 'the gateway into illegal drugs'.[108] A spate of legislative and administrative initiatives greatly strengthened the role of the federal authorities in dealing with drugs offenders. The Comprehensive Crime Control Act of 1984 gave government new powers of forfeiture, with the Anti-Drug Abuse Act of 1986 providing enhanced mandatory prison sentences for several federal illegal drugs offences. These statutes brought the federal government towards a pro-active role, often taking over from state and local efforts the tasks of arresting, prosecuting and imprisoning drugs offenders.[109] In terms of sentencing provisions, the US Sentencing Commission not only incorporated the Anti-Drug Abuse Act's penalty escalations into its guidelines, it added substantial increases of its own for drugs crimes. Between 1980-1992 the risk of imprisonment per drug arrest increased more than 400 percent, far greater than for any other offence during this period.[110] In the federal system fifty-six percent of prisoners in 1991 had been convicted of drugs offences, as had twenty-five percent of state prisoners, compared with twenty-five and six percent respectively in 1979.[111]

It is certainly the case, as Zimring and Hawkins have pointed out, that imprisonment rates for drugs offenses rose sharply after the Reagan war on drugs commenced, but this finding has to be seen within the context of an increasingly punitive climate. 'What happened in the 1980s to produce the explosion in drug imprisonment was an interaction between a shift toward "get tough" attitudes and an increasing volume of drug arrests.'[112] As these authors have pointed out, drugs arrests increased in the 1960s but were not accompanied by any substantial increase in imprisonment, and they caution that 'the belief that drug offenders should be sent to prison may simply reflect a belief that large numbers of all types of offenders should go to prison.'[113] There is, however, no question that the impact of this sustained offensive against drugs offenders has been especially devastating for black Americans. As Michael Tonry has demonstrated, all the indications were that drug usage was falling before the Reagan-Bush war on drugs was declared. This war 'destroyed lives of young, principally minority people in order to reinforce existing norms of young, mostly majority people.'[114]

Wilson contended that the distinction between prevention and law enforcement was artificial, claiming that 'law enforcement efforts can reduce demand as well as supply.'[115] He held that this ambiguity had clouded the debate over the Anti-Drug Abuse Act, and urged that efforts to reduce supply be directed more at local than at international markets, and more 'at controlling known users who are also predatory criminals or drug sellers' than at efforts to arrest 'Mr Big'.[116] With persistent heavy users 'we encounter the urban underclass in all its refractory and frightening complexity.'[117] His overall conclusion was simply stated: 'Only testing coupled with sufficient supervision and the willingness of the supervisor to revoke probation or parole and reincarcerate may be sufficient to reduce drug use and attendant criminality.'[118] While there were arguments in favour of decriminalizing drugs in terms of crime control these did not outweigh other considerations. 'The moral reason for attempting to discourage drug use is that the easy consumption of certain drugs is destructive to human character.'[119]

Wilson's restrained tone as co-editor of *Drugs and Crime* in 1990 contrasted with the aggressive style of an article entitled 'Crackdown' for *The New Republic* which he and John J DiIulio had written the previous year.[120] In order that drug dealers are taken off the streets for longer periods, it will be necessary to provide more prosecutors and judges, together with the provision of minimum security camps for lower level dealers. Wilson and DiIulio held that those who oppose incarceration or who are in favour of treatment as a means of reducing demand were wrong in whole or in substantial part. They added that even if these views were assumed to be correct they were irrelevant.

> At this stage, we are not trying to deter drug sales or reduce drug use. All we wish to do is to reassert lawful public control over public places . . . In the short run, this can be done by repeatedly arresting every suspected drug dealer and user and sending them through the revolving door. If we cannot increase the severity of the penalties they face, we can at least increase the frequency with which they bear them. In police terms, we want to roust the bad guys.

This would enable decent people to join with the police in regaining control of the streets.

> The greatest mischief is to assume that the demand for drugs will decline only when there is less racism and poverty, better schools and more jobs, more religion, and better quality television.[121]

BROKEN WINDOWS

In 1982, together with George L Kelling, Wilson published an influential article in *The Atlantic Monthly* entitled 'Broken Windows' which was to provide the basis for his approach to crime prevention. Wilson and Kelling contended that while many people were fearful of violence, especially sudden and violent attack by strangers, they were also afraid of 'being bothered by disorderly people. Not violent people nor, necessarily, criminals, but disreputable or obstreperous people: panhandlers, drunks, addicts, rowdy teenagers, prostitutes, loiterers, the mentally disturbed.'[122] Furthermore,

> (v)andalism can occur anywhere once communal barriers - the sense of mutual regard and the obligations of civility - are lowered by actions that seem to signal that no one really cares . . . Untended behaviour leads to the breakdown of community controls. A stable neighbourhood of families who care for their homes, mind each other's children, and confidently frown on unwanted intruders can change, in a few years or even a few months, to an inhospitable and frightening jungle.[123]

41

In brief, the Wilson-Kelling thesis is that 'disorder and crime are usually inextricably linked, in a kind of developmental sequence, by which unchecked rule-breaking leads to more serious street crime.'[124] Indeed, such areas are vulnerable to criminal invasion.

> The unchecked panhandler is, in effect, the first broken window . . . If the neighbourhood cannot keep a bothersome panhandler from annoying passersby, the thief may reason, it is even less likely to call the police to identify a potential mugger or to interfere if the mugging actually takes place.[125]

They added that 'the most important requirement is to think that to maintain order in precarious situations is a vital job . . . we must return to our long abandoned view that the police ought to protect communities as well as individuals . . . The police - and the rest of us - ought to recognize the importance of maintaining intact communities without broken windows.'[126] Wilson thereby disparaged policies favouring decriminalization and deinstitutionalisation because these failed 'to take into account the connection between one broken window left untended and a thousand broken windows.'[127]

Finally, Wilson and Kelling contended that although the police could effect 'incivilities', their capacity to do so had been reduced as a result of the downplaying of their public order duties. As Wesley Skogan has noted, towards the end of the 1980s there were some people who took the Wilson-Kelling thesis 'as a licence to recommend direct intervention by the police to break up disorderly activity and presumably intervene in the spiral of disorder, fear, crime and neighbourhood decline.'[128] However, when the model was tested in federally funded research projects in Newark and Houston, there were no discernable positive effects, although measures such as small shop-front police stations and encouraging officers to establish block watches did appear to have some success in reducing levels of perceived disorder and increasing levels of residential commitment. A leading expert on urban regeneration has concluded that the lack of empirical verification for the Wilson-Kelling thesis was not surprising.

> One underlying assumption is that cleaning up garbage and pushing out street people will better protect the neighbourhood from outsiders. This is oblivious to the simple truth that, in high crime inner-city neighbourhoods, perpetrators are just as likely to live next door or to be in one's own family than attack from outside perimeters. [129]

Two British criminologists, Tony Bottoms and Paul Wiles, have also taken exception to the politics of exclusion which appear to be inherent to the 'broken windows' thesis. They argued that this type of short-term crime prevention strategy may not be worth a massive increase in social divisiveness. In their view, the use of the concept of 'civility' had become distorted from its original meaning having to do with creating a more civilized society. The danger with the way the Wilson-Kelling thesis had been operationalized was that instead 'of locating its policies within a broader notion of the purpose of government', it had been 'transformed into a simple mechanistic theory of physical repairs and potentially petty social control'.[130] In similar vein, Elliott Currie's concern was that 'broken windows' led to a 'we-they' attitude, with offenders regarded as 'internal outsiders', and 'problematic people just further signs of local disorder, like litter or graffiti'. He argued that such ideas had been over-sold with the disturbing consequence that resources had been diverted 'away from other things we might do, while offering facile but easily dashed hopes that quick solutions will stop crime.'[131] 'Despite the up-by-the-bootstraps romanticism . . . much of it actually contains a profound pessimism about the possibilities of conscious social thinking at its core.'[132]

But for Wilson, the policy prescription remained straightforward:

Perhaps the first order of business for police and citizens alike is to identify the threatened but salvageable neighbourhoods and begin the attack on crime with an attack on offenses against public order - loitering drunks, public drug-dealing, aggressive panhandling, extensive littering and graffiti. These activities are not criminal in any serious sense, but they breed a fear of public places that can, if unchecked, reduce the extent to which citizens will feel confident about asserting their rights to be left in peace.[133]

WILSON'S CRIMINAL POLICY

At the 1991 Crime Summit the United States Attorney General, Richard Thornburgh declared: 'We are not here to search for the roots of crime or to discuss sociological theory.'[134] While James Q Wilson may have taken some satisfaction from this statement, he has tended to express disappointment at the gap between promise and realization with respect to criminal policy during the 1980s. His complaint has been that while much of what he has said has been applauded, he has

43

been aware of the degree to which it has been resisted in practice. 'In short', he wrote in 1983,

> the entire criminal justice system, from citizens to judges, is governed by perverse incentives . . . the principal problem facing policy-makers concerned about crime is how to rearrange those incentives to facilitate shared ends and to further systematic efforts to discover and implement new knowledge about how to best to attain those ends.[135]

It seems likely that Wilson would agree with John DiIulio's thesis that there have been two federal wars against crime: the first against poverty and the second (beginning in the 1980s) against criminals. In the first war the federal government played the major role; in the second, it attempted to encourage state and local government to bear the brunt of the action. With the arrival of Reagan the battle flag replaced the surrender flag. DiIulio concluded: 'During the second half of Bush's first (sic) term, a national political and intellectual consensus began to emerge that the second federal war on crime had failed, especially in relation to the urban drug and crime problem.'[136] Elsewhere, DiIulio stated that

> the record of federal crime policy from 1968 to 1992 is not highly encouraging. This is equally true for federal crime policy under Republican presidents and Democratic ones. The twin culprits have been, and continue to be, distributive politics and weak governmental administration. Policies are enunciated in rhetoric; but they are realized (or not) in action. Good ideas on crime prevention often get watered down by politically necessary compromises. Decent policies are poorly administered.[137]

A somewhat differen t assessment of this period has been provided by Michael Tonry, who believes that crime control policy has been debased. He contends that recent national administrations, on the basis of deceptive and distorted presentations of the data, have claimed that tough penalties have reduced crime.[138] Tonry is in no doubt as to which group of Americans have been least well served during this period.

> Contemporary crime control policies fundamentally impede the movement of disadvantaged black Americans into the social and economic mainstream of modern America . . . That our crime control policies have made the lives and life chances of that minority even worse than they otherwise would have been is shameful.[139]

Wilson, himself, has tended to be somewhat reticent about addressing issues of race and crime, although his search for genetic influences upon crime led him, with Richard Herrnstein, to conclude that '(t)he one factor that both seems clearly associated with offending and appears disproportionately among blacks is a low intelligence score.'[140] No such reticence, however, has been displayed by Wilson's colleague, John DiIulio who has argued that criminal justice policies had failed to protect black people. This follows from his thesis that America does not have a crime problem, but that inner city America does,

and that . . . no group of Americans would stand to benefit more from policies that kept convicted felons, adult and juvenile behind bars for all or most of their terms than crime-plagued black inner-city Americans and their children.[141]

Wilson is on record, along with DiIulio, as endorsing the placement of large numbers of the next generation of inner city youngsters in orphanages. However, unlike DiIulio, Wilson did not specifically refer to *black* youngsters in this context when he asked might not public funds be used 'to enable families in underclass neighbourhoods voluntarily to enrol their children, beginning at an early age, in boarding schools?' To which he added:

Suppose that unmarried mothers seeking welfare were given a choice: as a condition of receiving financial aid, they must either live with their parents or in group homes where they would be instructed in child care, receive a regular education, and conform to rules governing personal conduct and group responsibilities.[142]

These ruminations reinforce John DiIulio's contention that the core of Wilson's endeavours has been the exploration of the 'wellspring of civic virtue, the political and other conditions under which good citizens are produced, bad citizens are corrected, and desirable characters in general are made to flourish.'[143] 'Indeed, taken all in all' continued DiIulio, 'Wilson's criminology can be read as a brilliant note on the philosophy of civic virtue . . . His seminal contributions to the field of criminal justice are all attempts to identify and establish in late twentieth-century America a *"form of order"* (Aristotle) that promotes civic virtue.'[144]

The year before the Crime Commission issued its report, Wilson wrote in *The Public Interest* that Americans were unlikely to be pacified by crime statistics, even when these were accurate. He thought it was possible that the issue of 'crime in the streets' might become the major domestic issue of the far right, replacing "communist subversion" and even "socialism". A less implausible or rigid candidate than Barry Goldwater could make such an issue - with its obvious implications for . . . intellectuals who want to "mollycoddle" or "explain away" immorality - a major element in a serious bid for power. This is not a problem about which American liberalism has hitherto had much to say . . . But unless liberalism can show an eagerness to cope with this problem - even if it means spending more money on larger police forces - it will become a notable victim of crime in the streets.[145]

Wilson's mission to meet this challenge and chart a new way forward for criminal policy had begun, albeit with rapidly receding traces of a liberal perspective.[146]

ENDNOTES

1. President's Commission on Law Enforcement and the Administration of Justice, *The Challenge of Crime in a Free Society* (Washington DC, US Government Printing Office, 1967), 58.

2. As Mayer's summary of the polling data makes clear, over the twenty years from the mid-1960s, support for greater severity in the sentencing of offenders increased by almost 40 percentage points. See, William G Mayer, *The Changing American Mind, How and Why American Public Opinion Changed between 1960 and 1988* (Ann Arbor, The University of Michigan Press, 1992), 263 and tables at 258-364.

3. Abt Associates, *American Prisons and Jail, Volume 1, Summary Findings and Policy Implications* (Washington DC, US Government Printing Office, 1980), 14.

4. Ronald Bayer, 'Crime, Punishment, and the Decline of Liberal Optimism', *Crime and Delinquency,* 27 (1981), 190.

5. Daniel P Moynihan, *Maximum Feasible Misunderstanding, Community Action in the War on Poverty* (New York, The Free Press, 1970), liii-liv.

6. Wilson was an adviser to Crime Commission on police and on science and technology. At the time he was associate professor of government at Harvard and director of the Joint Centre for Urban Studies of MIT and Harvard, having succeeded Daniel Moynihan in that position.

7. James Q Wilson, *Thinking About Crime* (New York, Basic Books, 1975), 68.

8. ibid. 56; Lloyd Ohlin was director of research for the President's Crime Commission while on leave from Columbia University. From 1967 until his retirement in 1982 he was the Roscoe Pound Professor of Criminology at Harvard Law School. Together with colleagues at the Centre for Criminal Justice at Harvard Law School he conducted a large-scale study of the closure of young offender institutions in Massachusetts. See, for example, Alden D Miller and Lloyd E Ohlin, *Delinquency and Community, Creating Opportunities and Controls* (Beverly Hills, Sage, 1985).

9. Richard A Cloward and Lloyd E Ohlin, *Delinquency and Opportunity: A Theory of Delinquent Gangs* (New York, Free Press, 1960); see also, Peter Marris and Martin Rein, *Dilemmas of Social Reform, Poverty and Community Action in the United States* (New York, Atherton Press, 1967), and Moynihan, op. cit. n. 5.

10. Unpublished paper by Lloyd Ohlin to the 1973 American Sociological Association meeting (cited by Wilson, op. cit. n. 7, at p. 240).

11. op. cit. n. 7, p. 70.

12. For example in 1976 Wilson wrote that he regretted 'the Americanization of English criminal justice', by which he meant that Home Office civil servants had

47

failed to learn from the mistakes made by their opposite numbers in the United States. 'There is scarcely a single ill-advised recommendation of the President's Commission on Law Enforcement and Administration of Justice that the British Home Office and its various advisory councils do not seem determined to repeat.' James Q Wilson, 'Crime and Punishment in England', *The Public Interest*, 43 (1976), 5.

13. See, James Q Wilson, *Negro Politics, The Search for Leadership* (Glencoe, III, Free Press, 1960); and Edward C Banfield and James Q Wilson, *City Politics* (Cambridge, Massachusetts, Harvard University Press and the MIT Press, 1963).

14. 'Entering Criminology through the Backdoor', address by James Q Wilson to the American Society of Criminology, cited in, John J DiIulio, 'James Q Wilson and Civic Virtue', *Political Science*, 24 (1991), 750.

15. op. cit. n.7, p. xi-xii; see also, James Q Wilson, *Varieties of Police Behaviour* (Cambridge, Massachusetts, Harvard University Press, 1968).

16. On Wilson's writings on policing, see for example, his study with Barbara Boland in which he argued, on the basis of a cross-sectional study of 35 large American cities, that as the proportion of robberies resulting in arrest rises, the rate at which robberies are committed falls. This crime reduction was also associated with more aggressive police patrolling; see, James Q Wilson and Barbara Boland, 'The Effects of the Police on Crime', *Law and Society Review*, 12 (1978): 367-390.

17. See, James Q Wilson, *The Moral Sense* (New York, Free Press, 1993).

18. John J DiIulio is Professor of Politics and Public Affairs, Princeton University. His PhD thesis, supervised by Wilson, was published as *Governing Prisons: A Comparative Study of Correctional Management*, (Glencoe III, Free Press, 1987).

19. op. cit. n.14, p. 751.

20. Wilson's extensive political science output includes *Political Organizations* (1973), *The Investigators* (1978), *Bureaucracy* (1989) and the leading textbook, *American Government*.

21. James Q Wilson, op. cit. n.7, p. 68.

22. Benedict Alper, 'Thinking About Crime', *Crime and Delinquency*, 22 (1976), 487.

23. Published at about the same time as *Thinking About Crime* was Ernest van den Haag's *Punishing Criminals* (New York, Basic Books, 1975), but this book despite its tough message failed to make anything like the same impact.

24. John J DiIulio op. cit n. 14, p. 751.

25. Almost thirty years later, in the footsteps of his mentor, John J DiIulio published a piece entitled 'Let 'em Rot' (*Wall Street Journal*, January 26, 1994). The origins of the other chapters of *Thinking About Crime* (1975) were *The New York Times Sunday Magazine* (3), *Commentary* (2), *The Public Interest* (2), and *Atlantic Monthly*. A further chapter drew from two essays which had appeared in book form.

26. For a recent example, see Jock Young, 'Incessant Chatter: Recent Paradigms in Criminology' in Mike Maguire, Rod Morgan and Robert Reiner (eds), *The Oxford Handbook of Criminology* (Oxford, Oxford University Press, 1994), esp. 97-102. In this chapter Young draws out parallels between 'left realism' and 'right realism'.

27. Charles E Silberman, *Criminal Violence, Criminal Justice* (New York, Random House, 1978), 221.

28. Paul Rock, Review of 'Thinking About Crime', *British Journal of Criminology*, 19 (1979), 80-1.

29. Jerome H Skolnick, 'Are More Jails the Answer?', *Dissent*, 25 (1976), 96-7.

30. op. cit. n. 7, p. xviii.

31. Wilson had departed from a viewpoint expressed in 1969, when he was quoted as saying: 'I hold us responsible (for recidivism) for insisting that the only way to deal with offenders is to lock them up in some bucolic retreat behind high walls in the countryside, not recognizing that if we isolate them from the community, their attitude toward the community will wreak a terrible price on us when, as they will be eventually, they are released.' (*New York Times Magazine* (May 11, 1969). The article was based upon the transcript of a discussion on crime issue which also involved James Vorenberg, who had served as executive director of the Crime Commission.

32. op. cit. n. 7, p. xv.

33. ibid., 55.

34. ibid., 59. Edwin H Sutherland and Donald R Cressey, *Principles of Criminology* (Philadelphia, Lippincott, 1966). This standard text was in its seventh edition at the time. See n. 9 re Cloward and Ohlin.

35. op. cit. n. 7, pp. 61-62.

36. James Q Wilson, 'The Political Feasibility of Punishment' in J Cederblom and William Blizek (eds), *Justice and Punishment* (Cambridge, Mass., Ballinger, 1977), 122-123.

37. op cit n. 7, pp. 235-6.

38. James Q Wilson, 'Crime and the Liberal Audience', *Commentary*, 51 (1971): 71-78. A later version appeared in his *Thinking About Crime* (1975).

39. op. cit. n. 7, p. 84.

40. op. cit. n. 36.

41. James Q Wilson, 'Crime and American Culture', *The Public Interest*, 70 (1983), 46.

42. op. cit. n. 7, pp. 222-223.

43. ibid., 234.

44. As Attorney General in the Johnson Administration, Ramsey Clark was much derided on the 'law and order' issue by Richard Nixon during the 1968 presidential campaign. Nixon went on to beat Hubert Humphrey in the first campaign in which crime had featured prominently. On Clark's vision of criminal policy, see Ramsey Clark, *Crime in America. Observations on its Nature, Causes, Prevention and Control* (New York, Simon and Schuster, 1970).

45. James Q Wilson, 'On Crime and the Liberals', *Dissent*, 33 (1985), 223.

46. ibid. 224.

47. Elliott Currie, 'Reply to James Q Wilson', *Dissent*, 33,(1985), 229.

48. Michael Tonry, *Malign Neglect - Race, Crime and Punishment in America* (New York and Oxford, Oxford University Press, 1995), 119.

49. James Q Wilson, '"Policy Intellectuals" and Public Policy', *The Public Interest*, 64 (1981), 33.

50. ibid., 32.

51. ibid., 33.

52. Hugh Hecklo, 'Reaganism and the Search for a Public Philosophy' in John L Palmer (ed), *Perspectives on the Reagan Years* (Washington, DC, The Urban Institute Press, 1986), 40.

53. ibid., 50.

54. op. cit. n. 49, p. 31.

55. ibid., 43; compare Roger Hood's conclusion. '(T)he belief that expert advice based on criminological and penological research is the foundation for penal change, is only a screen behind which ideological and political factors, perhaps inevitably, shape those attitudes which imbue legislation.' Roger Hood, 'Criminology and Penal Change: A Case Study of the Nature and Impact of some recent Advice to Governments', in Roger Hood (ed), *Crime, Criminology and Public Policy, Essays in Honour of Sir Leon Radzinowicz* (London, Heinemann, 1974), 417.

56. Governor Edward King had been elected as the conservative Democratic governor of Massachusetts on a 'tough on crime' mandate. His early decision to set up a task force on youth crime was widely regarded as an attempt to reverse the progress made in the state towards deinstitutionalisation. The task force was established in October 1980 and reported in April 1981. It was chaired by Judge James Nixon and in addition to Wilson its other members included Judge Francis Pointrast who was a longstanding opponent of Dr Jerome Miller who had closed down the state's young offenders institutions in the early 1970s. The task force recommended more use of locked facilities, longer sentences and for more juveniles to be tried in adult courts. But as Miller later commented, it was too late. 'The money had left the institutional grounds. Youth corrections was largely in the hands of private, nonprofit agencies who delivered services to the youth. The old system couldn't be resurrected without grave political consequences.' Jerome G Miller, *Last One Over the Wall. The Massachusetts Experiment in Closing Reform Schools* (Columbus, Ohio, Ohio State University Press, 1991), 217; see also Andrew Rutherford, *Growing out of Crime* (Winchester, Waterside Press, 1992), 66-93; the Reagan administration task force on violent crime is discussed below.

57. James Q Wilson and Richard J Herrnstein, *Crime and Human Nature, The definitive study of the causes of crime* (New York, Simon and Schuster, 1985).

58. See especially, David J Rothman, 'The Horrors of Prison Reform', *The New York Review of Books* (February 17, 1994), 34-38.

59. op. cit. n.7, p. 198.

60. Alfred Blumstein, Jacqueline Cohen and Daniel Nagin, *Deterrence and Incapacitation* Report of the National Academy of Sciences Panel on Deterrent and Incapacitative Effects (Washington, DC, National Research Council, National Academy Press, 1978).

61. James Q Wilson, *Thinking About Crime*, revised edition (New York, Basic Books, 1983), 137.

62. ibid., 143.

63. ibid., 145

64. Ten years later Wilson contended that chronic offenders accounted for 'as many as 75% of offenses'. op cit. n. 57, p. 144.

65. Marvin E Wolfgang, Robert M Figlio and Thorsten Sellin, *Delinquency in a Birth Cohort* (Chicago, University of Chicago Press, 1972), 252.

66. Shlomo Shinnar and Reuel Shinnar, 'The Effects of the Criminal Justice System on the Control of Crime: A Quantitative Approach', *Law and Society Review*, 9 (1975), 607-608. By *safety* crime, the authors are refering to 'crimes that affect a person's safety'. ibid, 582. For critiques of the Shinnars' model, see for example, Rudy Haapeanen, *Selective Incapacitation and the Serious Offender,*

A Longitudinal Study of Criminal Career Patterns (New York, Springer-Verlag, 1990), 6-7; and, Franklin E Zimring and Gordon Hawkins, *Incapacitation. Penal Confinement and the Restraint of Crime* (New York and Oxford, Oxford University Press, 1995), 267.

67. op. cit. n. 7., p. 225.

68. op. cit. n. 60, p. 76.

69. Gerald R Ford, *A Time To Heal, The Autobiography* (New York, Harper Row, 1979), 269. President Ford's proposals, which went to Congress in June 1975, included mandatory prison sentences for federal offences committed with firearms or other dangerous weapons, as well as for certain drugs trafficking offences.

70. It was later Wilson's view that these programmes would have been more effective if they had made use of the predictive criteria developed by researchers at the RAND Corporation. Peter W Greenwood and Allan Abrahamse, *Selective Incapacitation, Report prepared for the National Institute of Justice* (Santa Monica, California, Rand Corporation, 1982). Instead, 'in practice career criminal units have employed criteria that focus largely on criminals in the twilight of their careers, bypassing the offenders likely to inflict the most harm on society'. op. cit. n. 61, 175.

71. Attorney General's Task Force on Violent Crime, *Final Report* (Washington, DC, US Department of Justice, 1981). The task force was set up by the Attorney General, William French Smith, under the co-chairmanship of former Attorney General Griffin Bell and Governor James R Thompson of Illinois. The other members were David L Armstrong, president of the District Attorneys' Association, Frank G Carrington, Crime Victims Legal Advocacy Institute, Robert L Edwards, Director of the Division of Local Law Enforcement of the Florida Department of Law enforcement, William L Hart, police chief of Detroit and Wilbur F Littlefield, the Public Defender for Los Angeles County. The executive director was Jeffrey Harris, a former assistant US Attorney. The Task Force reported within its mandate of 120 days. Phase I (measures that the Department of Justice could implement immediately) was presented within 60 days. The final report was published on August 17, 1981.

72. ibid., 2.

73. James Q Wilson, (ed), *Crime and Public Policy* (San Fransisco, California, 1983).

74. op. cit. n. 71, p. 2.

75. Barbara Boland and James Q Wilson, 'Age, crime and punishment', *The Public Interest*, 51 (1978), 23.

76. Two unnamed members of the task force were against this recommendation on the grounds that predicting dangerousness was not sufficiently accurate. Wilson had set out his own views two years later when he supported a proposal of

Steven Schlesinger (director designate of the Justice Department Bureau of Statistics) on removing the exclusionary rule and changing the bail rules. op. cit. n. 73, p. 280. The Bail Reform Act of 1984 permitted pre-trial detention to protect 'the safety of the community' based upon factors which included the nature of the threat posed. The legislation was upheld by the Supreme Court in *The United States v. Salerno* (1987).

77. op. cit. n. 71, p. 76.

78. Governor Thompson's remarks were at a news conference at the time the report was released, and are quoted in Diane R Gordon, *Doing Violence to the Violence Problems A Response to the Attorney General's Task Force* (Hackensack, New Jersey, National Council on Crime and Delinquency, 1981), 7. Among the task force's other recommendations was the call for further research 'programs designed to speed the prosecution of career criminals which grew directly out of basic research on who commits how many offenses, and these programs, in turn, were subjected to objective evaluations to discover which aspects of them were or were not contributing to enhanced public safety.' Well organized programs by prosecutors to identify and give special prosecutorial attention to these career criminals can help ensure a speedy trial, a high probability of conviction, and a substantial sentence for such offenders; it commented that 'the decision is a management determination wholly within the prosecutor's discretion, and the defendant has no particular rights at stake'; there should be additional federal investigative and prosecutorial resources to combat youth gangs, and the task force saw no need to have separate federal funds directed at juveniles. It also suggested that federal military bases be used for prison expansion; that victim impact statements be provided to courts; prosecutors to fully inform courts of all circumstances relevant to sentencing decisions; a clear and consistent enforcement policy with regards to narcotics and dangerous drugs; a waiting period for purchase of handguns was endorsed (but this did not widen the limitations on handgun ownership); support was given to sentencing provisions in the Criminal Code Reform Act (The Code provisions constituted a 'truth-in-sentencing' package that will inform both the public and the offenders of the real penalty being imposed on each defendant).

79. Alan R Gordon and Norval Morris, 'Presidential Commissions and the Law Enforcement Assistance Administration' in Lynn A Curtis (ed), *American Violence and Public Policy, An Update of the National Commission on the Causes and Prevention of Violence* (New Haven and London, Yale University Press, 1985), 129.

80. Michael Gottfredson and Travis Hirschi, 'The True Value of Lambda would Appear to be Zero: An Essay on Career Criminals, Criminal Careers, Selective Incapacitation, Cohort Studies, and Related Topics', *Criminology*, 24 (1986), 216.

81. ibid. 217.

82. ibid., 231.

83. op. cit. n. 70.

84. op. cit. n. 61, p. 151.

85. Marcia R Chaiken and Jan M Chaiken, 'Offender Types and Public Policy.' *Crime and Delinquency*, 30 (1984), 220.

86. Mark H Moore, Susan R Estrich, Daniel McGillis and William Spelman, (eds), *Dangerous Offenders, The Elusive Target of Justice* (Cambridge, Massachusetts and London, Harvard University Press, 1984), 185. In their final report Moore and his colleagues provided a qualified endorsement of selective policies of incapacitation, which they considered should be guided by a very narrow definition of dangerousness, be thought of as primarily retributivist rather than utilitarian, ie targeted on those whose acts have revealed them to be particularly blameworthy rather than on those who are predicted to behave badly in the future, and finally that such policies only address a portion of the overall problem of criminal justice (ibid., 182-183).

87. op. cit. n. 61, p 159.

88. Alfred Blumstein, Jacqueline Cohen, Jeffrey A Roth, and Christy A Visher (eds.), *Criminal Careers and 'Career Criminals'*, Volume 2 (Washington, DC, National Research Council, National Academy Press, 1986), 206.

89. ibid., 352.

90. Peter W Greenwood and Susan Turner, *Selective Incapacitation Revisited, Report prepared for the National Institute of Justice* (Santa Monica, California, Rand Corporation, 1987), 48.

91. Andrew von Hirsch, *Past or Future Crimes, Deservedness and Dangerousness in the Sentencing of Criminals* (New Brunswick, NJ, Rutgers University Press, 1985), 15.

92. op. cit. n. 61, p. 160.

93. James Q Wilson, 'Prisons in a Free Society', *The Public Interest*, 117 (1994), 40.

94. Franklin E Zimring and Gordon Hawkins, *The Scale of Imprisonment* (Chicago and London, University of Chicago Press, 1991), 112.

95. See, for example, Franklin E Zimring and Gordon Hawkins 'The Growth of Imprisonment in California', *British Journal of Criminology*, 34 (1994), 87-91.

96. According to one careful observer, 'mandatory sentencing laws since 1975 have been America's most popular sentencing innovation. By 1983, 49 of the 50 states had adopted mandatory sentencing for offenses other than murder or drunk driving.' Michael Tonry, 'Mandatory Penalties' in Michael Tonry and Norval Morris (eds), *Crime and Justice, A Review of Research* (Chicago and London, University of Chicago Press 1992), 251. Wilson was, of course, a member of the task force which had recommended mandatory prison sentences for the use of a firearm in the commission of a federal felony. The philosophy of mandatory

minimum sentencing did not emerge only from notions of incapacitation but also from 'a crime control model based on just punishment, deterrence and incapacitation that holds the offender fully accountable and yields penalties commensurate with conduct severity'. *The Federal Sentencing Reporter* (Jan/Feb 1993).

97. op. cit. n. 91, p. 9.

98. US Department of Justice, *Prisons and Prisoners in the United States* (Washington, DC, Bureau of Justice Statistics, 1992), 1.

99. op. cit. n. 7, p. 86.

100. op. cit. n. 73, pp. 279-280

101. James Q Wilson, 'Drugs and Crime', in Michael Tonry and James Q Wilson (eds), *Drugs and Crime: Crime and Justice, A Review of Research,* Vol 13 (Chicago and London, University of Chicago Press, 1990), 543.

102. Arnold S Trebach, *The Heroin Solution* (New Haven and London, Yale University Press, 1982), 344.

103. James Q Wilson, Mark H Moore and I David Wheat, 'The Problem of Heroin', *The Public Interest*, 29, (1972): 3-28. This article was updated for both editions of *Thinking About Crime.*

104. op. cit. n.7, p. 178.

105. op. cit. n. 27, p. 234.

106. James Q Wilson and Robert L Dupont, 'The Sick Sixties' *The Atlantic Monthly*, 232 (1973): 91-98. This article was revised for the first edition of *Thinking About Crime.*

107. op. cit. n.7, p. 20.

108. Robert L Dupont quoted in Arnold S Trebach, 'The Loyal Opposition to the War on Drugs. Drugs and the Criminal Law in Western Democracies.' in Jan van Dijk, Charles Haffmans, Frits Rüter, Julian Schutte and Simon Stolwijk (eds), *Criminal Law in Action. An overview of current issues in Western societies* (Deventer, Kluwer Law and Taxation Publishers, 1988), 224.

109. John J DiIulio, Steven K Smith, and Aaron J Saiger, 'The Federal Role in Crime Control' in James Q Wilson and Joan Petersilia, (eds), *Crime* (San Fransisco, California, Institute for Contemporary Studies, 1995), 445-457.

110. Marc Mauer and Tracy Huling, *Young Black Americans and the Criminal Justice System: Five Years Later* (Washington, DC, The Sentencing Project, 1995), 10.

111. op. cit. n. 48, p. 113.

112. op. cit. n. 95, p. 89.

113. op. cit. n. 94, p. 116.

114. op. cit. n. 48, p. 97. Michael Tonry's overall judgement on the Reagan-Bush wars on illegal drugs is unequivocal. He writes that 'there were no valid bases for believing that the war would accomplish its ostensible objectives, that the claim to protect black victims was disingenuous, and that there is no arguable basis for justifying the war's malign neglect of its implications for black Americans.' (ibid., 105).

115. op.cit. n. 101, p. 527.

116. ibid., 533.

117. ibid., 529.

118. ibid., 541.

119. ibid., 523.

120. James Q Wilson and John J DiIulio, 'Crackdown. Treating the symptoms of the drug problem.' *The New Republic*,(201):21-25.

121. ibid., 24

122. James Q Wilson and George L Kelling, 'Broken Windows: The police and neighbourhood safety', *The Atlantic Monthly,* 249 (1982): 29-38; 'panhandler' is American slang for a beggar.

123. ibid., 31-32.

124. ibid.

125. ibid., 34.

126. Ibid., 38.

127. Ibid., 35.

128. Wesley G Skogan, 'Disorder, crime and community decline.' in Tim Hope and Margaret Shaw, (eds), *Communities and Crime Reduction* (London, HMSO, 1988), 50.

129. Elliott Currie, 'The March of Folly - Crime and the Underclass.' in Tim Hope and Margaret Shaw (eds), *Communities and Crime Reduction* London, HMSO, 1988), 198; see also, Lynn A Curtis, *American Violence and Public Policy, An Update of the National Commission on the Causes and Prevention of Violence* (New Haven and London, Yale University Press, 1985).

130. Anthony E Bottoms and Paul Wiles, 'Crime and Housing Policy: a Framework for Crime Prevention Analysis' in Tim Hope and Margaret Shaw (eds), *Communities and Crime Reduction* (London, HMSO, 1988), 95-96.

131. Elliott Currie, 'Two Visions of Community Crime Prevention', in Tim Hope and Margaret Shaw (eds), *Communities and Crime Reduction* (London, HMSO, 1988), 284.

132. ibid., 284-285.

133. op. cit. n. 73, p. 283; it is instructive to compare the article by Wilson and Kelling with remarks on 'aggressive beggars and squeegee merchants' in September 1995 by the British shadow home secretary, Jack Straw. See also *A Quiet Life, Tough Action on Criminal Neighbours* (London, the Labour Party, 1995).

134. US Department of Justice, *Attorney General's Summit on Law Enforcement Responses to Violent Crime: Public Safety in the Nineties* Conference Summary, (Washington, DC, 1991), 7.

135. op cit. n. 73, p. 289.

136. John J DiIulio, 'Crime' in Henry J Aaron and Charles L. Schultze (eds), *Setting Domestic Priorities: What can Government Do?* (Washington, DC, Brookings, 1992).

137. John J DiIulio, 'Crime in America: Three Ways to Prevent It'. Typescript of Congressional Testimony, (20 January, 1995), 20.

138. op. cit. n. 48, p.6. Tonry took John J DiIulio to task for his 'Let 'Em Rot' piece in the *Wall Street Journal* (26 January, 1994), remarking that: 'Perhaps the most extreme claims about the threatening nature of prisoners were made by John DiIulio of Princeton University, who ought to know better.' (ibid., 26).

139. ibid., 208-209.

140. op. cit. n. 57, p. 470. But Wilson and Herrnstein went on to ask why the homicide fatality rate among black males nearly doubled between the early 1960s and 1973, increasing from 34.3 per 100,000 to 65.8. They, however, dismissed the possibility that this increase could be 'wholly or even largely explained by purely genetic factors'. (ibid., 472).

141. John J DiIulio, 'The Question of Black Crime.' *The Public Interest*, 117, (1994), 15.

142. James Q Wilson, 'In Loco Parentis. Helping Children When Families Fail Them', *The Brookings Review*, (Fall 1993) 14-15; see also James Q Wilson, 'Time To Bring Back the Orphanage?' *The Sunday Times* (London, 4 December, 1994).

143. op. cit. n. 14, p. 748.

144. ibid., 751-752.

145. Reprinted as James Q Wilson, 'The Nature and Extent of Crime in the United States' in Marvin R Summers and Thomas E Barth (eds) *Law and Order in a Democratic Society* (Columbus, Ohio, Charles E Merrill, 1970), 14-15.

146. In his book, *The Amateur Democrat* Wilson wrote that he was 'a member of the same generation and I come from the same educational background of the Amateur Democrat . . . Like them, I was once lured into an amateur democratic club in order to ring doorbells for Adlai Stevenson. That was several years ago, and my views on this kind of activity have changed considerably.' James Q Wilson, *The Amateur Democrat Club Politics in Three Cities* (Chicago and London, University of Chicago Press, Revised edition, 1966), xiii.

CHAPTER 3

Managerialism and Credibility

For many years after the Second World War, The Netherlands was regarded as a model of the liberal humanitarian approach to criminal policy. Much scholarly attention focused upon the post-war years during which the Dutch prison population fell from 6700 to 2350 between 1950-1975, or from 66 to the extraordinarily low rate of 17 per one hundred thousand inhabitants.[1] A working ideology had from the 1950s developed among prosecutors and the judiciary, central to which was 'the distinctly negative value placed upon imprisonment, which is viewed, at best, as a necessary evil, and, at worst, as a process likely to inflict progressive damage on a person's capacity to re-enter the community.'[2]

For more than a generation, this anti-penal frame of reference had been articulated by a handful of scholars at the Institute of Criminology within the Law Faculty at Utrecht University, who were 'primarily motivated by a strong empathy with the delinquent as a fellow human being.'[3] The formidable driving force of the Utrecht School was comprised of W P J Pompe, a criminal law scholar, P H Baan, director of the Psychiatric Observation Clinic, and G Th. Kempe, a criminologist. A fourth member of the School was R Rijksen, whose critical study of the prison system, *Prisoners Speak Out*, caused a considerable stir when it was published in 1958.[4] As Contantijn Kelk had commented, the essential theme of the Utrecht School was 'an emphasis on the offender's own responsibility and on punishment as a means of making good the offence to society, after which rehabilitation could take place.'[5]

The Utrecht School not only had a profound impact upon the working ideology of a generation of lawyers, but it was influential within central government and across the criminal justice process. While the Utrecht School was not, as David Downes has carefully concluded, the source of anti-penal thinking in The Netherlands, it reinforced such thinking over at least two decades. These and other Dutch élites had 'a distinct appreciation of the extent to which community tolerance cannot be taken for granted, but needs active elicitation and encouragement.'[6] It is important to underline the proactive stance taken by the criminal justice élites in promoting this wider tolerance. Downes has correctly observed that the reductionist approach pursued at that time in The Netherlands seemed 'to derive not so much from a free-floating tolerance on the part of the people in general but from the convictions of the most influential élites that crime is best combatted by social and institutional, rather than specifically penal, means.'[7]

The notion of criminal policy received very little attention in the Netherlands until the late 1960s. As Kelk has pointed out, *belied*, the Dutch word for policy, was originally associated with wise choices and was only later used to cover action, rules and regulations.[8] Auguste C 't Hart has suggested that it was not until the second half of the 1960s that any real need was felt for a coordinated criminal policy, and that it had been prompted in part by the widescale social protests of that decade from which there emerged a crisis of confidence in criminal justice arrangements among large sections of the population.[9] The most evident outcome was the initiative taken by the prosecution service, the *Openbaar Ministerie* (OM), which after reviewing the results of its activities decided to give more weight to the public interest presumption *not* to prosecute. This reassertion of the expediency principle was also extended to decision-making by police officers at the earlier stage of the process. From 1973 onwards, 'tripartite arrangements' were established in order to encourage the coordination of policy between the OM, the police and local authorities. According to 't Hart, it was a severe shortage of resources which compelled the OM to establish priorities in the development of its policy, and, '(a)s policy developed, the OM had a tendency to encourage centralization and to expand its own influence.'[10]

Developments proceeded in this fragmentary way until the government white papers of 1985 and 1990 further consolidated OM's policy-setting role. As Julia Fionda, a British scholar, has recently observed, 'throughout the sweeping policy changes of both the 1980s and 1990s, the prosecutor has consistently emerged as "the winner", the key figure in the criminal process.'[11]

By the end of the 1970s it was clear that the new shape of criminal policy had sharply departed from the tolerant attitudes of the previous generation. Most notably, beginning in 1975, prison numbers began to steadily rise and by the mid-1980s it was clear that the transformation of Dutch criminal policy was of one of profound dimension. As Antonie Peters of Utrecht University observed, 'many of the earlier humanitarian ideals have been lost in a drift towards business-like, centralized, bureaucratized and efficiency-oriented policies in which financial and quantitative considerations loom larger than the philosophy of resocialisation.'[12] The dominant concerns were policy

60

planning and organization, with the criminal law regarded as one among several means of social control available to the state. 'This entails a concept of the law', Auguste 't Hart told the same international conference in 1988, 'which gives precedence to instrumentalism, at the expense of the notion of the law as an intrinsic value, and to functional rationality at the expense of substantial rationality.'[13] In similar vein, Kelk protested that a 'quantitative approach to criminal justice reigns supreme, serving in the first place the interests of the Ministry of Justice, while individualization of the penal law centred around the offender as a human being is being pushed ever further back.'[14] Commenting upon the changing political climate since the mid-1970s, Simon Stolwijk observed: 'Gone is the calm and quiet attitude to the rise in crime in the sixties. Gone too is the idea that the most restrained criminal law is the best criminal law.'[15] He contended that contemporary developments were no longer characterised by the idea that custodial sentences are an evil as such, and that 'without a convincing ideology it is impossible to reduce the use of prison.'[16]

As a means to exploring selected aspects of this rapid reshaping of criminal policy in The Netherlands, particular attention is given to the influential role of Dato Steenhuis who throughout the 1980s moved between senior posts within the prosecution service and the Ministry of Justice. Although a large number of academics and practitioners were influential during this period, it was Steenhuis who first articulated and actively promoted the new and distinctively managerial perspective within the Dutch criminal justice context. Referring to Steenhuis' use of the commercial company as a metaphor for the criminal justice system, René van Swaaningen has commented that Steenhuis 'turned out to have the perfect nose for the spirit of the time'.[17] Dato Steenhuis studied law at Groningen University where he remained to take his doctorate within the Institute of Criminology under Professor Wouter Buikhuisen. In 1977 he joined the staff of the Research and Documentation Centre (RDC) within the Ministry of Justice, which at that time was directed by Buikhuisen. Two years later Steenhuis succeeded to the directorship of the RDC and remained in that post until 1982. At about the time he joined the RDC, Steenhuis published his doctoral dissertation, in which he argued that fines should replace imprisonment as the standard sentence for drunken drivers. This proposition was consistent with the post-war anti-penal thinking and, as David Downes has suggested, it may have given further solace to the sceptical view of prisons shared by many judges.[18]

Within two or three years, Steenhuis extended his scrutiny to a wider arena. Writing about the police, he noted that if the prosecution service's new interest in the formulation of criminal policy was to be successfully realised, closer cooperation with the police was a requisite. He therefore regretted that the police and prosecuting authorities were resisting efforts in this direction, both agencies apprehensive about losing autonomy and influence.[19] Three years later, after highlighting 'the interaction of the various components' of criminal justice, he stressed in similar vein the need to bring into line the workings of the various subsystems. 'It frequently happens', he complained, 'that one part of the system undoes the work of another.'[20]

Without question, Steenhuis' most influential publication was a two-part article which appeared in *Delikt en Delinkwent* in 1984, under the title 'The workings of criminal justice: a small step back and a huge leap forward'.[21] The opening sentence, 'the system of upholding the law is not doing very well', encompassed what had become Steenhuis' preoccupation. The police, prosecution service and the prison system were all under-resourced. 'Altogether then, the picture that we have is of a system that is bursting at the seams . . . ' He noted that his conclusions were consistent with a recent contention by the Minister of Justice that there was 'a lack of a legal system that is able to uphold the law.'[22] But to reach any conclusion it was necessary to know what purposes were served by criminal justice. As far as Steenhuis was concerned, the way ahead simply flowed directly from his analogy of criminal justice as a factory or commercial enterprise.

> The criminal justice company (hereafter, SRB) can, in my opinion, be defined as the totality of organs whose function, in mutual relationship to one another, is aimed at (or responsible for) the maintenance of the penal legal order. The different production phases of the company are coupled to each other serially, like a car manufacturing factory or in a company where for example chocolate bars are produced.

This analogy of criminal justice as a commercial company, Steenhuis noted, fitted comfortably with an increasingly instrumentalist conception of the criminal law.

In exploring differences between a commercial company and the SRB, Steenhuis noted that reported offences (analogous to the supply of raw materials) could only be partially controlled. Furthermore, the SRB lacked a centralised management, and each of the different 'production phases' had separate or even completely independent directors. If the judiciary were left out of the picture, the minister of justice might be regarded as the managing director. But control of the police rested with mayors and the minister of justice was thereby unable to decide the level of input into the SRB. However, these and other differences did not prevent Steenhuis from concluding that the production processes were essentially the same: the serial production of a certain end-product, with the execution of the previous production phases providing the input into the next stage. The SRB's ultimate objective was to influence the people so that their behaviour conformed to penal norms. He argued that while all the activities within the SRB did not specifically aim at punishment, nonetheless, they shared this common goal. Because of the serial nature of the production process, room for manoeuvre became more restricted in the later phases of sentencing and administration of punishment.

Steenhuis distinguished between three client or 'target' groups, which he characterised as: conformists, potential offenders and offenders.[23] For people to remain conformists they needed, from time to time, to be reminded that society as a whole thinks as they do. This group required 'norm-conformation', which was achieved by taking action against those who broke the law. In the absence of such action by the authorities, these people gradually would be more inclined to become potential offenders. But for potential offenders, norm-conformation is not enough, because 'what distinguishes them from real offenders is that the potential of punishment stops them from breaking the law.' As far as the offenders were concerned, they received too much attention. Given these three groups of clients, the SRB produced three versions of its end product: for conformists it produced norm-confirmation; for potential offenders it produced the threat of punishment; and for actual offenders it produced actual punishment. He argued that the SRB had focused unduly on punishment to the detriment of the two other versions of the SRB's end product. Consequently, there needed to be a different allocation of production means within the organization so as to give more attention to the other two groups of clients.

Citing Dutch criminal statistics for 1982, Steenhuis noted that there were 900,000 offences recorded by the police, on the basis of which some 200,000 cases were then referred to the prosecutor. Of these, 45% were put before a court, and in 9% of the cases dealt with by the courts the judge did not reach a verdict. Steenhuis declared that 'any real-life production firm that dealt with its production means in such a way would have become bankrupt a long time ago.' A way forward was to prioritise serious offences, but this would exacerbate the situation regarding less serious offences. For example, with respect to bicycle theft he concluded that 'it is at least clear that the SRB is unable to organize its production in a way which determines which norms will or will not hold in the long run.' Output (adherence to the law) might be increased through a better use of the threat of punishment and norm-conformation, which in turn could be achieved by increasing the visibility of the SRB. But this required a better working relationship between the police and the prosecutor.

Interviewed ten years later, Steenhuis said:

It is difficult to recall when the seeds of this kind of thinking were put into my mind. When I finished working at the RDC in 1982 and became a deputy prosecutor general, from having had a very tight schedule with many discussions with people from abroad, I was in a small room in Leeuwarden doing appeal cases and having, in my opinion, a great deal of time to think about what we were doing in the criminal justice system. That might have been the moment I started putting things together which might have been in my head but had not realized before that time. Between 1983-84, I became responsible for running policy courses for prosecutors from all over the country. These were two-day conferences for groups of about fourteen persons and we were teaching them something about management: setting problems as to how to set priorities in dealing with crime problems. That was the practical beginning of this sort of thing, and because of my close enquiries into these things I began to think about bringing all the knowledge from these people together. From these courses we gradually developed the idea of a criminal justice chain. This was not a new idea because in 1969 Alfred Blumstein[24] had talked about the criminal justice system in such a way.'[25]

Although a gradual abandonment of the liberal humanitarian consensus on Dutch criminal policy had been evident since the late 1970s, the coup de grace was the Ministry of Justice's white paper, *Samenleving en Criminaliteit*, [Society and Criminality, A Policy Plan For The Years To Come], published in May 1985.[26] The white paper has been represented as 'a fundamental break with the lenient tradition in our country',[27] and the plethora of official publications which appeared in its wake over the next decade simply reinforced the depth of the transformation. The immediate origins of the white paper lay in a motion in the Second Chamber of the States on 11 October 1984 for a policy plan to improve the maintenance of law and order, which in turn was

motivated by a growing concern among the population over the increase in crime, by the fear of a loss of confidence on the part of the public in government and its role as the protector of private and public interests and by the fear of a further erosion in the citizen's conception of standards and in social control.[28]

The problem and its solution, as defined by the authors of the white paper, were simply stated:

> The gap between the number of infringements of standards embodied in the criminal law and the number of real responses to them by the criminal justice authorities has become unacceptably wide. The criminal justice system must be placed in a position, once it has initiated interventions at least to bring them to a credible conclusion. Order must be restored in the affairs of criminal justice. It must always be possible to execute sanctions imposed and to do so without undue delay.[29]

It can be seen that the document's language occasionally betrayed a distinctly sharp tone, in asserting that 'order must be restored in the affairs of criminal justice. It must always be possible to execute sanctions imposed and to do so without undue delay'[30] and 'The administration of criminal justice is, in a way which is apparent to everyone, no longer able to react adequately to serious violations of the law by proper means of judicial intervention.'[31] The white paper's aim, 'to restore and strengthen the credibility of law enforcement', found expression in specific proposals, most notably to reduce by fifty percent the use of unconditional waivers by the prosecution service and in the decision to further increase the number of prison cells. One close observer regarded the huge investment in the prison system as being the most significant feature of a decisive escalation of the overall criminal justice process.[32]

Society and Crime was the first comprehensive effort in The Netherlands to articulate a statement of national criminal policy. Indeed, the white paper might be viewed as an unusual attempt to create an integrated criminal policy through a synthesis of criminal justice reform and a variety of crime prevention initiatives.[33] The attention given to crime prevention largely derived from recommendations pressed upon the government by an on-going committee on petty offences under the chairmanship of a member of the Lower House, Dr H J Roethof.[34] The white paper endorsed the committee's package of social and situational crime prevention measures. These were intended to strengthen the bonds between young people and society by enhancing the quality of life within the family, school, work and recreation; improve surveillance of public spaces by reintroducing jobs such as caretakers of apartment blocks, sports-coaches and ticket inspectors; and finally, to encourage the planning and construction of built-up areas so that normal surveillance was not obstructed. As John Blad has observed, the interim report of the Roethof committee reached back to the earlier period of leniency, insisting that penal repression could only do more harm than good, and should be limited therefore to a subsidiary role of reinforcing norms. The authors of *Society and Crime*, however, 'fitted the policy lines of the Roethof Committee into a more encompassing framework', which implied a *volte face* with respect to the fundamentals of Dutch criminal policy.[35] As two other academic observers commented, although the section of the white paper which dealt with petty crime was based upon the Roethof report, the white paper gave a more instrumentalist and judicial orientation to the committee's recommendations. 'So whereas Roethof's focus was at the level of the neighbourhood, schools and clubs, the emphasis of the white paper was on a new trilateralism between local government, the police and the public prosecutor.'[36]

The white paper's main theme, however, was driven less by the promotion of crime prevention than by anxieties concerning the effectiveness of criminal justice agencies. It is in this respect that Dato Steenhuis' contribution to the white paper is particularly evident. He has described his relationship to the group of officials who drafted the white paper:

> I was not in the Ministry of Justice at the time of the white paper but working as a prosecutor. Normally speaking, prosecutors would not be invited to participate in working on this kind of white paper, and there was no-one else at my level involved in these discussions. It may have been because of my 1984 article that I was invited to participate. Another reason may have been because I had already worked in the Ministry. I remember meeting with some high civil servants from the Ministry in a hotel in the middle of the country where we sat for about three days producing a draft. Whether this was the first or second draft I don't remember, and I should make it clear, that I was not allowed to participate in the decision-making as to how the final draft was agreed. But the ideas that I developed in that article had their influence in the white paper. So began the thinking of the "justice chain".[37]

The authors of the white paper also followed Steenhuis in contending that criminal justice had been too one-sided in dealing with law-breakers, at the expense of the other two target groups. 'Citizens for whom the observance of the rules of criminal justice is more or less self-evident as well as those who are incidental or potential offenders should be included in the target group . . . '[38] There are two main elements, therefore, of criminal policy: crime prevention and making the administration of criminal justice more credible. With regard to crime prevention, it was concluded that addressing 'underlying causes' held forth little promise, and James Q Wilson was cited as the authority on this point.[39] As far as 'enhancing the standards-reinforcing effect of the administration of justice' was concerned, the white paper proposed that a key strategy was halving the number of unconditional waivers by prosecutors over the next five years. This would 'ensure that the criminal justice system can function as a credible end-link in the preventive chain of efforts on the part of the public at large and the local government administrators working together with the public prosecution service through integrated plans for the control of petty crime.'[40] In addressing the means by which these changes might be brought about, the influence of Steenhuis becomes especially transparent.

> The first step which needs to be taken in restoring the credibility of the administration of criminal justice is to eliminate the innumerable stoppages in the criminal justice system, so as to ensure that cases are dealt with and concluded systematically and within a reasonable timescale. *In order to gain an understanding of the problems which arise in these processes, it is appropriate to present the totality of activities of the criminal justice system, in the form of a conceptual model, as a factory with a continuous production point.* [41]

Steenhuis' 'Huge Leap Forward' was cited at this point in the text. After reviewing the various stages of the process, the white paper went on to state that

> this somewhat stylized picture of the system gives a clear impression of the mutual interdependence of the various organs in the administration of criminal justice. In other words the activities of the various components of the machine of criminal justice must be adjusted to one another as effectively as possible in order to guard against the production of "semi-finished products" (charges and court judgments) which ultimately cannot be processed by the system.[42]

Auguste 't Hart was particularly struck by the white paper's insistence that crime had to be tackled 'by means of a very complicated operation, in which various sectors of government policy and the actions of various government bodies have to be coordinated . . . criminal law and criminal law policy are viewed as purely instrumental.'[43] More recently he noted that, when viewed in this way, the criminal justice system had to be a coherent and consistent crowning piece to a comprehensive policy of combatting crime, which is conceived as an enormous organizational problem in terms of the adjustment and coordination of the management divisions of different ministries.[44]

In 'Huge Leap Forward', Steenhuis also urged that the prosecution service, which occupied a central position within the SRB, should assume responsibility for policy coordination. But Steenhuis cautioned that if the OM were to effectively exercise this sort of controlling role at the regional and national level of government it would need to be much better informed. It would have to understand not only how to influence criminal behaviour, but also gain an appreciation of the conditions necessary for penal actions to be successful. If the OM were to be able to rationalise its own 'production process', it had to be granted overall responsibility for suggesting the optimal policy choices. In order to carry out this ambitious role, the OM would need to acquire good information about the effectiveness of all criminal justice agencies. The white paper followed Steenhuis in recommending that the prosecution service should take on the task 'of ensuring consistency within the criminal justice system.'[45] Steenhuis remained a powerful advocate in favour of OM assuming a strong coordinating role. Three years later, he noted that there were still only about 300 prosecutors compared with 40000 police officers, and that the police had, in the words of a senior officer, enjoyed 'a free hunting-ground'. 'However,' commented Steenhuis, 'the prosecutors are on their way back.'[46] He went on to note how the situation of the prosecution service had changed considerably during the decade.

From a body only dealing with cases reported to it by the police it has evolved to an important organ of criminal policy. Perhaps even *the* most important because . . . the public prosecutor is at the very centre of the criminal justice system and, at the same time, has (formal) authority over the policy, is able to control the input of the judiciary and is also responsible for the execution of sentences.[47]

Observing the growth of power by the OM, Constantijn Kelk has noted, but with less equanimity than Steenhuis, that the prosecution service has played a very central and probably initiating role in the movement towards a managerial conception of criminal justice.[48]

In September 1986, Steenhuis took advantage of a high profile opportunity to set forth his views at an international conference in Amsterdam marking the Centenary of the Dutch Criminal Code. He observed that the Dutch criminal law had acquired a reputation throughout the world for its mild and humane nature, so much so in fact that foreigners are sometimes inclined to talk with a certain affection of those simple-minded Dutchmen who still believe in the goodness of man.[49]

He did not mince his words in declaring that

despite the favourable picture abroad, the coordination between the different links in the criminal justice system was so deficient that the functioning of the system as a whole was seriously impaired and the credibility of the criminal justice system was being undermined.[50]

He asked why there was so little agreement as to the objectives of the criminal justice system? Despite some progress following *Society and Crime*, the entire 'production process' was still too much geared towards the offender at the expense of the two other 'target groups', potential offenders and the public at large. The '3:1 package' was not working, and as a consequence potential offenders were more likely to commit crime. He added that the required expansion of resources had not occurred, and that in all its various phases the Dutch criminal justice system remained exceptionally mild and humane. Although Steenhuis, along with the authors of *Society and Crime,* seemed to accept that there should not be a fundamental expansion of the criminal justice system, in his next breath he asked whether in other circumstances there should not be some system of flexible adjustment in line with 'the increased demand for its products'. It was his firm conviction that

if demand for "safety" understandably increases, it is unacceptable that this demand should not be met solely because it is not politically expedient to reallocate government funds on a flexible basis, for instance because the Minister of Education considers that the share of education in central government funds should remain constant notwithstanding a sharp drop in the number of pupils.[51]

Furthermore, Steenhuis was far from convinced that the cultural differences of the police, prosecutor and local government would be overcome by the tripartite consultative arrangements. He believed that more far-reaching changes were required, including the creation of a 'common organizational culture'. Whereas a coherent underlying philosophy had been responsible for the success of Japanese industry, as far as criminal justice in The Netherlands was concerned, to date there has been a complete absence of a coherent philosophy, although *Society and Crime* has proposed a number of clear premises on which such a philosophy could be based. What is important from the point of view of integration here is how the various parts of the criminal justice system can be induced to operate on the basis of such a philosophy or such premises. Minzberg (sic) speaks quite openly in this connection of "indoctrination".[52]

What was required included a common training course (assessment would be based on a model geared very closely to the idea of integration of criminal justice; anyone failing to meet the standards of the course would have to leave); there also needed to be a 'rotation of personnel, with the exception of the judiciary, across the criminal justice process'; and finally, persons holding senior posts would be encouraged to always keep in view the whole of the criminal justice system rather than the vantage point of their own agency.

Steenhuis was reluctant to place any normative constraints upon his managerial perspective of criminal justice. He was directly pressed to do this in the late autumn of 1986 when he expounded his managerial vision of criminal policy to a Council of Europe criminological research seminar on *Interactions within the Criminal Justice System*. In his paper, Steenhuis did not shrink from describing the context in alarming terms: 'The walls of the criminal justice system-building, once a stable rock in a society morally in decay, are tottering.'[53] Looking across the experience of a number of European countries, he observed that the percentage increase of the case load decreased at each further stage in the criminal justice system. He presented data on trends in The Netherlands between 1975-84 demonstrating 'a lasting decrease of the "coverage" of crime by the criminal justice system'.[54] All of this amounted to 'a major threat for the functioning of the criminal justice system and its credibility'.[55] If resources fail to keep up with the number of cases, unsatisfactory mechanisms may come into play. 'The Criminal Justice System is irresolute and undecided. It behaves like a child in a sweet shop unable to choose between the lollipop, the candybar or the liquorice.'[56] For good measure, he added that

the flow of cases through the criminal justice system can be compared with the flow of any physical product through the different phases of the production process.[57]

Steenhuis was pressed at this international gathering to think through the implications of his model for the protective and human rights aspects of criminal policy. Did not fragmentation serve these normative purposes? He rejected the view that more cooperation and better coordination led in the direction of George Orwell's *1984*.

> This fragmentation may indeed be desirable as far as protection of the rights of individuals is concerned. At the same time however it is substantially impeding an effective and efficient administration of criminal justice and thus a waste of limited public resources.[58]

While acknowledging the philosophical underpinnings of fragmentation, his concern was about the breakdown of the '3:1 package' since the mid-1960s, with the result that 'norms start to become blurred in the minds of the conformists, particularly if they are victims.'[59] Steenhuis' distinction between the law-abiding citizen (regarded as the conformist and partner of government) for whom the social contract protects his interests and the suspect, for whom there is the status of civil death once expelled from the social contract, was subsequently challenged by Auguste 't Hart who held that this carried with it the inevitable consequence that politicians will always declare that precedence be given to the respectable citizen.[60]

Steenhuis returned to the question as to what normative limits should be placed upon his managerial model in an essay he wrote in honour of his former professor and colleague, Wouter Buikhuisen. He argued that there was

> an imbalance between what the government has to offer the individual when he breaks the law and what it has to offer to the one who abides by it . . . the imbalance has led to quite disastrous consequences: judicial authorities are faced with a blurring of standards in many areas and with a loss of credibility.

The criminal law must be applied efficiently if its credibility were to be maintained.

> Efficiency is also called for in the sense that measures taken to protect the position of the suspect and which are out of all proportion to the aims of the law should be open to discussion. Not every measure which weakens the position of the suspect needs to be seen as a direct attack on the constitutional state, as is often suggested, nor even do a number of measures taken consecutively. The constitutional state does not only serve the suspect, but every other individual too.[61]

In 1990 the Ministry of Justice published *Law in Motion* as a five year follow-up to *Society and Crime*. Steenhuis has acknowledged his

71

impact upon the 1990 paper, highlighting the section which established a target for prosecutors' offices in terms of dismissals and the imposition of community service orders by the courts. He commented that from 'a concrete point of view, my influence on the 1990 paper was greater, although from a theoretical point of view my ideas for the 1985 white paper might have been more important.'[62] The 1990 white paper, *Law in Motion*, scorned what was regarded as the legacy of the 1960s and 1970s.

> From being a traditionally fairly conventional country, The Netherlands witnessed the adoption of a very tolerant attitude, best characterized by the modern catchphrase "why not", not only towards alternative forms of dress but also towards pornography, squatting, illegal copying of gramophone records and drug abuse.[63]

It also noted the considerable progress made in meeting targets set five years earlier. In particular, unconditional waivers by prosecutors had been reduced by 50%, and the extensive prison building programme had proceeded as planned. But the authors of *Law in Motion* considered that 'legal care' remained under considerable pressure, as illustrated by the results of a survey conducted in 1989 showing that 85% of Dutch nationals over 18 believed crime to be a 'very serious problem'. Furthermore, the white paper asserted that compared to other countries, the 'criminal law enforcement ratio' in The Netherlands had fallen to a 'very low level'.[64] The government therefore announced that it aimed to substantially increase the enforcement ratio for the various categories of criminal offence including burglary. The authors of *Law in Motion* stated: 'The concept of credibility in the context of the administration of criminal law should not be confused with severity. Criminal sanctions derive their credibility in part from their educational value.'[65] It was also noted that major problems ahead included the enforcement of democratically established rules and tackling a crime rate which remained unacceptably high. 'What is at stake is nothing less than the credibility of constitutional government and its democratic and social values.'[66] Furthermore, there would need to be a considerable expansion in the OM in the years ahead if it were to be successful in ensuring 'the social effectiveness of the criminal justice system'.[67]

A trenchant critic, Auguste C 't Hart has characterised the 1990 white paper as taking a blinkered view of the law and society. Freed of traditional social controls and exhibiting a strong individualistic ethos together with an ambiguous attitude to the law, the problem is regarded as the individual citizen. By contrast, the government's role

72

is considered to be 'a success story in difficult times'. He argued that everything which did not support this particular view was left out of account, including other perspectives on societal developments, the effectiveness of the strategy set out in the 1985 white paper, and the credibility of the victim surveys upon which he relied. He also had considerable doubts about the rationale, associated with Steenhuis and taken forward in the 1990 white paper, that the 'steering' role of the public prosecution service should be further strengthened.[68]

A slightly different note was hinted at in the first policy plan to be produced by the prosecution service, *Strafrecht met belied*, which appeared within a few days of *Law in Motion*. The OM plan stated:

> In our constitutional state a few important demands have been made on criminal law enforcement. One of these demands is that there is a legal standard and there are legal guarantees to such an extent that it is sufficient. This implies a constant watch to what extent the status of the suspect and of the people who give them legal aid are being protected. It also implies that criminal law enforcement is able to offer the legal protection, which citizens can reasonably ask for. It also implies that enough attention should be paid to the status of victims of offenses.[69]

In OM's plan, Auguste 't Hart detected a broader conception of 'the enforcement of the law', with the term embracing not only the combatting of crime but also the requirement of legal protection.[70] This theme was reinforced in 1992 with an Easter Letter from the procurator-generals to the Minister of Justice and to Parliament. The significance of this letter arises from the heightened strains in the relationship between OM and the ministry of justice. *Strafrecht met belied* and the Easter Letter from the procurator-generals suggest that within the prosecution service there was in the early 1990s a growing sense that a corrective was required to the managerial orientation of the Ministry of Justice. To the extent that this was the case, Steenhuis' impact upon criminal policy had peaked by the end of the 1980s.[71]

Steenhuis, as one of the country's most senior prosecutors in the 1990s, has continued to be an influential operator. Responsible for an area which covers the provinces of Leeuwarden, Groningen and Assen, he was described in a 1994 newspaper article as being able to act

> on his own initiative and give his opinion - something which Steenhuis loves to do . . . In mapping out and coordinating the prosecution process, Mr Dato Steenhuis has taken clear control . . . (he) has no problem being tough in his judgement about the *penal business* in The Netherlands.

Steenhuis owes the patent to this term. In the past it used to happen that people said to him "Long live the *penal business* man".[72]

The overall pattern during the first half of the 1990s has continued to be one of further encroachments by managerialism. Within the prison system, for example, there has been a move to decentralise operations to governors with many services becoming eligible for privatisation, and

> the prisons will actually be transformed into companies themselves, in the sense that they will have to produce a measurable "output" and will be organized according to the bloodless norms and mathematical formula(s) of efficiency bureaux.[73]

The Ministry of Justice paper, *Werkzame Detentie*, published in 1994, stated that it took for its starting point 'the change in the demands on the prison system *in terms of the integrated crime policy in the law enforcement chain*.'[74] During the 1980s, according to two leading commentators, 'The Netherlands has consistently moved towards a purely numerically legitimated penitentiary policy, in which only management considerations really count.'[75] Despite the huge prison building programme, the sharp rise of the prison population during the 1980s undermined the rule of one person to a cell. In July 1994, after 'the never ending laments, mainly from the Public Prosecution Service about the shortage of prison-capacity' the resistance to cell sharing was finally broken.'[76]

The new managerial tone was also evident with reference to the probation service. The Ministry of Justice reduced the budget for social work and after care needs and shifted the focus to producing reports for the judiciary and prosecution. René van Swaaningen and his colleagues have commented that

> Dato Steenhuis, who has, as the highest official of the Prosecution Service (OM), the special task to coordinate sanctioning policy, currently even claims that the probation service is primarily a service for the prosecution. The organization of the probation service is already modelled after his favourite model as a production-unit of the "penal chain".[77]

In the movement towards more restrictive non-custodial penalties, an experiment in electronic monitoring, having been rejected in 1990, started four years later in Leeuwarden, the prosecutorial jurisdiction managed by Steenhuis.[78]

dominently political approach has no intrinsic limits."[18] Elsewhere, with Gerard de Jonge, van Swaaningen has asked:

(W)here indeed would be the limits of instrumentalism? It has been the strongest point of the post-war Dutch penal reformers that they actually did pose such functional and normative questions, and in respect to the intellectual level of the debates and the genuine social concern in those days, the complacent disdain and cynical book-keeper's logic of current policy makers seems quite inappropriate.[19]

ENDNOTES

1. Andrew Rutherford, *Prisons and the Process of Justice* (Oxford, Oxford University Press, 1986), 136-143.

2. Willem de Haan, *The Politics of Redress. Crime, Punishment and Penal Abolition* (London, Unwin Hyman, 1990), 68.

3. Willem de Haan 'Abolitionism and the Politics of "Bad Conscience"', *Howard Journal of Criminal Justice*, 26 (1987), 19.

4. R Rijksen, *Meningen van Gedetineerden over de Strafrechts-pleging* [Prisoners Speak out] Assen, van Gorcum, 1958).

5. Constantijn Kelk, 'Criminal Justice in the Netherlands' in Phil Fennell, Christopher Harding, Nico Jorg, and Bert Swart (eds) *Criminal Justice in Europe. A Comparative Study* (Oxford, Oxford University Press, 1995), 1.

6. David Downes, *Contrasts in Tolerance, Post-War Penal Policy in the Netherlands and England and Wales* (Oxford, Oxford University Press, 1988), 205.

7. ibid. 205.

8. op. cit. n. 5, p. 7.

9. Auguste C 't Hart, 'Criminal Law Policy in The Netherlands' in Jan van Dijk, Charles Haffmans, Frits Rüter, Julian Schutte and Simon Stolwijk (eds), *Criminal Law in Action* (Deventer, Kluwer Law and Taxation Publishers, 1988), 74.

10. ibid., 79.

11. Julia Fionda, *Public Prosecutors and Discretion: A Comparative Study* (Oxford, Oxford University Press, 1995), 130.

12. Antonie A G Peters, 'Main Currents in Criminal Law Theory' in Jan van Dijk, Charles Haffmans, Frits Rüter, Julian Schutte, and Simon Stolwijk (eds) *Criminal Law in Action. An overview of current issues in Western Societies* (Deventer, Kluwer Law and Taxation Publishers, 1988), 32.

13. op. cit. n. 9, p. 86.

14. op. cit. n. 5, p. 18.

15. Simon A M Stolwijk, 'Alternatives to Custodial Sentences' in Jan van Dijk, Charles Haffmans, Frits Rüter, Julian Schutte and Simon Stolwijk (eds), *Criminal Law in Action. An overview of current issues in Western societies* (Deventer, Kluwer Law and Taxation Publishers, 1988), 289.

16. ibid., 291.

17. René van Swaaningen and Gerard de Jonge, 'The Dutch Prison System and Penal Policy in the 1990s. From humanitarian paternalism to penal business management' in Mick Ryan and Vincenzo Ruggierro (eds), *Western European Penal Systems; A Critical Anatomy* (London, Sage, 1995), 43.

18. op. cit. n. 6, p. 203.

19. Dato Steenhuis, 'Experiences in Police Effectiveness: The Dutch Experance' in R V G Clarke and J M Hughes (eds), *The Effectiveness of Policing* (Aldershot, Gower, 1980), 127-130.

20. Dato Steenhuis, L C M Tigges and J J A Essers, 'The Penal Climate in The Netherlands, Sunny or Cloudy?' *British Journal of Criminology*, 23 (1983), 14.

21. Dato Steenhuis, 'Strafrechtelijk Optreden: stapje terug en een sprong voorwaarts' [The working of criminal justice: a small step backward and a huge leap forwards'] *Delikt en Delinkwent,* 14, (1984), 395-414, 497-512. Hereafter referred to as 'Huge Leap Forward'; the excerpts which follow were translated for the author.

22. For background on the Minister of Justice's Explanatory Memorandum to the 1984 budget, see 't Hart who noted: 'Following the commotion caused by the critical report of the General Chambers of Audit for 1981, the Minister of Justice admitted in the explanatory memorandum to the budget estimates of his ministry for 1983 that unless action were taken unacceptable situations would occur. In the 1984 explanatory memorandum, the position was described as alarming, especially as regards petty crime. The minister stated that even though the criminal justice authorities should intervene only when this would have a desired social effect, the criminal law, together with other systems of enforcement, must nevertheless guarantee a minimum level.' op. cit. n. 9, p. 81.

23. Jan van Dijk has commented that Steenhuis' three target groups bear a close resemblance to his own threefold framework of primary, secondary and tertiary offender - oriented crime prevention. Jan J M van Dijk, 'Crime Prevention Policy: Current State and Prospects' in Gunther Kaiser and Hans-Jörg Albrecht (eds) *Crime and Criminal Policy in Europe. Proceedings of the 11. European Colloquium* (Freiburg, Max-Planck Institute, 1990), 215.

24. Alfred Blumstein and Richard Larson, 'Models of a Total Criminal Justice System', *Operations Research,* 17 (1969): 199-231. In the mid-1960s, when Blumstein was with the Institute for Defense Analysis, he served as director of the science and technology task force for the President's Crime Commission. See especially, the chart showing 'A general view of the Criminal Justice System' in President's Crime Commission, *The Challenge of Crime in a Free Society* (Washington, DC, US Government Printing Office, 1967, 8-9.

25. Interview with Dato Steenhuis, November 1994.

26. Ministry of Justice, *Samenleving en Criminaliteit* (The Hague, Ministry of Justice, 1985); the shortened English version, *Society and Crime, A Policy Plan for The Netherlands* is relied upon here; hereafter 'Society and Crime'.

27. John R Blad, 'Selected Issues on Crime and Punishment in The Netherlands' (unpublished paper, Erasmus University, Rotterdam, 1992), 7.

28. op. cit. n. 26, p. 1.

29. ibid., 20.

30. ibid.

31. ibid., 31.

32. Willem de Haan, 'Explaining Expansion: the Dutch Case' (paper presented at the thirteenth Conference of the European Group for the Study of Deviance and Social Control, Hamburg, September 1985), 2.

33. Jan van Dijk (who was an advisory member of the committee) has defended the white paper in terms of providing such a synthesis, as 'it seems obvious to bring about a vigorous expansion in the capacity of the various constituent parts of the criminal justice system'. At the same time the government agrees with the Roethof Committee, 'that petty crime is essentially the result of underlying social problems for which the criminal law is not the appropriate mode of approach in the first instance'. Jan J.M. van Dijk and Josine Junger-Tas, 'Trends in Crime Prevention in The Netherlands in Tim Hope and Margaret Shaw (eds) *Communities and Crime Reduction*, London, HMSO, 1988, 264). Jan van Dijk was also closely involved in drafting *Society and Crime*, and is described by two observers as being the 'genius' behind it. Jolande uit Beijerse and René van Swaaningen, 'Social Control as a Policy: Pragmatic Moralism with a Structural Deficit', *Social and Legal Studies*, 2 (1993), 284. A leading British criminologist welcomed the white paper, regardless of any views as to its substance, as representing 'an integrated criminal justice policy' which he compared to the rather 'ineffectual way in which British governments over the years have attempted a similar task'. A Keith Bottomley, 'Blue-Prints for Criminal Justice: Reflections on a Policy Plan for the Netherlands.' *Howard Journal of Criminal Justice*, 25 (1986), 200. Bottomley had in mind Home Office statements on criminal justice issued in 1977 and 1984, and which are discussed in Chapter 4.

34. The committee, which was been set up in September 1983 by the then minister of justice, F Korthals Altes, presented an interim report in December 1984 and its final report in June 1986. Its members included Dr Hirsch Ballin, at that time professor of constitutional and administrative law at the Catholic University, Tilburg, and later minister of justice.

35. op. cit. n. 27, p. 7.

36. Beijerse and van Swaaningen, op. cit. n. 33, pp. 283-284.

37. Interview with Dato Steenhuis in November 1994; Steenhuis added that by 1985 the climate in The Netherlands had already become tougher on crime. This tendency was obscured by the white paper and only became apparent when Ernst Hirsch Ballin became minister of justice in 1989. For example, in a speech to new judges on 1 April 1993 Ballin stated that the citizen no longer asked primarily for the legal protections afforded to his individual rights but for the protection of collective interests against attacks. This implied that a new balance had to be struck between the credibility and the serious maintenance of social norms the one hand, and legal guarantees for the individual on the other. Mr Ballin invited the new judges to be moral entrepreneurs and to adapt to the sentiments which currently are felt by the public at large. Cited by René van Swaaningen, 'The Moral Revival as Meta-Narrative of Law and Order in The Netherlands for the 1990s.' (Unpublished paper presented at the University of Kent, 1993), 4.

38. op. cit. n. 26, p. 22.

39. James Q Wilson (ed.), *Crime and Public Policy* (San Francisco, Institute for Contemporary Studies, 1983).

40. op. cit. n. 26, pp. 30-31.

41. ibid., 40 (emphasis added).

42. ibid., 37.

43. op. cit. n. 9, p. 96.

44. Auguste C 't Hart, *Openbaar Ministerie en Rechtshandhaving, Een verkenning* [Public Prosecution and Law Enforcement, An Exploration] (Arnhem, Gouda Quint, 1994).

45. op. cit. n. 26, p. 38. The white paper also referred to the setting up of a joint working group of members of the public prosecutors department and officials of the Justice Ministry to strengthen consistency within the criminal justice system; this issue is set out in much detail in Chapter 4 of the full version.

46. Dato W Steenhuis, 'Criminal Prosecution in The Netherlands' in J E Hall-Williams (ed), Role of the Prosecutor, (Aldershot, Gower, 1988), 52.

47. ibid., 54.

48. op. cit. n. 5, pp. 8-9.

49. Dato W Steenhuis, 'Coherence and Coordination in the Administration of Criminal Justice' in Jan van Dijk, Charles Haffmans, Frits Rüter, Julian Schutte and Simon Stolwijk *Criminal Law in Action An overview of current issues in Western societies* (Deventer, Kluwer Law and Taxation Publishers, 1988), 220.

50. ibid. 230.

51. ibid. 237.

52. ibid., 243-244. Steenhuis' reference is to Henry Mintzberg,*The Structuring of Organizations* (Englewood Cliffs, Prentice Hall, 1979).

53. Dato W Steenhuis, 'Problems of Coordination and Cooperation in Daily Practice Between the Different Agencies of the Criminal Justice System', in *Interactions Within the Criminal Justice System* (Seventeenth Criminological Research Conference, Strasbourg, Council of Europe, 1986), 10. Steenhuis prefaced this observation with a quotation from the British home secretary, Leon Brittan's introduction to his *Criminal Justice: A Working Paper* of 1984, and from his own minister of justice in the explanatory memorandum to the Ministry of Justice budget for 1984. At a planning meeting in May 1985 Steenhuis and others were involved in discussions as to the general topic and selection of rapporteurs and allocation of tasks. The author served as the conference's general rapporteur.

54. ibid., 13.

55. ibid., 16.

56. ibid., 17.

57. ibid., 20.

58. ibid., 21.

59. ibid., 25.

60. op. cit. n. 44, p. 226.

61. Dato W Steenhuis, 'Individual Rights and Collective Interests in the Application of the Criminal Law' in Josine Junger-Tas and Irene Sagel-Grande (eds), *Criminology in the 21st Century. A collection of essays presented to Professor Wouter Buikhuisen* (Leuven/Apeldoorn, Garant, 1991), 159.

62. Interview with Dato Steenhuis, November 1994.

63. Ministry of Justice, *Law in Motion. A policy plan for Justice in the years ahead* (The Hague, Ministry of Justice, 1990), 15; for a later example of the Dutch government's views on the 1960s generation, see report of a conference held on 17 March 1994, organized by the research department of the Ministry of Justice, and which concluded: 'After the anti-authoritarianism of the 1960s and 70s, a turning point in thinking about crime was reached by the beginning of the 1980s. Punishing is again "allowed", and the legitimation of penal sanctions is no longer solely sought in its resocialising effect, but again in incapacitation and retribution as well.' Cited in op. cit. n. 17, p. 40.

64. ibid., 40.

65. ibid., 43.

66. ibid., 85.

67. ibid., 51-52.

68. op. cit. n. 44. The 1990 white paper drew upon a controversial study of victimization based upon telephone interviews in several countries. Jan van Dijk , Patricia Mayhew and M Killias, *Experiences of Crime Across the World. Key Findings of the 1989 International Crime Survey* (Deventer, Kluwer Law and Taxation Publishers, 1990). For a summary of critiques of this study see, René van Swaaningen, John Blad and Reinier van Loon, *A Decade of Criminological Research and Penal Policy in the Netherlands. The 1980s: the era of business-management ideology* (Centre for Integrated Penal Sciences, Erasmus University Rotterdam, 1992), 42-43.

69. Openbaar Ministerie, *Strafrecht met belied: Beleidsplan Openbaar Ministerie 1990-1995* (The Hague, Openbaar Ministerie, 1990), 15. There is a pun here with 'belied' meaning policy but also ʻtreading carefully'.

70. op. cit. n. 44. pp. 13-15.

71. René van Swaaningen and colleagues in their review of criminological research during the 1980s did detect one or two 'emerging impulses' that they thought might 'grow towards a counter-movement against the present business-management ideology . . . ' op. cit. n. 68, p.93.

72. *Vru Nederland*, 15 January, 1994.

73. op. cit. n. 17, p. 26.

74. Ministry of Justice, *Werkzame detentie* [Effective Detention, Summary and Implementation], (The Hague, Ministry of Justice, 1994), 3; The official English version is title obscures the pun on *werkzame* which means both effective and hard labour.

75. op. cit. n. 33, p. 139.

76. op. cit. n. 17, p. 4; it was determined by Royal Decree of 8 July 1994 but could not be enacted until 20 July because of resistance from prison authorities; ibid, 9. The government plans were for a total prison system capacity of 13,000 by the end of 1996, a five-fold increase since the mid-1970s.

77. ibid., 10.

78. René van Swaaningen and Jolande uit Beijerse, 'From Punishment to Diversion and Back Again: The Debate on Non-Custodial Sanctions and Penal Reform in The Netherlands.' *Howard Journal of Criminal Justice*, 32 (1993): 136-156.

79. Dato W Steenhuis 'Over kwaliteit en sturing binnen het strafrechtelijk bedrijf' [Quality and Steering within the Criminal Justice System] in A Cachet (ed), *Reorganisatie van de Polite: Een tussenbalans* (Arnhem, Gouda Quint, 1992)

80. Considerable scepticism about OM's increasingly powerful position was also evident at a national conference which took place in 1994, organized by Hans de Doelder of Erasmus University Rotterdam.

81. van Swaaningen *et al*. op. cit. n. 71, pp. 56-57.

82. ibid., 93.

83. René van Swaaningen, 'Het confectiepak van product-manager Justitia.' *Recht en Kritkiek* 21 (1995): 13-37.

84. op. cit. n. 17, p. 40.

CHAPTER 4

Principled Pragmatism

For most of the post-war period, the direction of criminal policy in Britain reflected a broad consensus across the main political parties. The actual shaping of policy was largely in the hands of senior civil servants within the Home Office, one of whom once wrote of 'the diverse, and what one might almost say haphazard, character of the process'.[1] This 'backstage' activity was essentially pragmatic in orientation rather than driven by formulated principles.[2] The occasional departures from this traditional posture, such as the abrupt and premature dissolution in 1964 of the Royal Commission on the Penal System, could be read as warnings to anyone seeking to strike a way forward that owed more to principle than to practicalities of the moment. Above all, the 'still centre'[3] of the Home Office carried forward an extraordinarily varied workload but little in the way of obvious long-term purpose.

Early in 1974 some tentative steps had been taken to establish a planning organization within the Home Office in response to a sense within the Heath Government that the themes of policy might be welded into an overall strategy with specified objectives.[4] Three years later, the Crime Policy Planning Unit completed and published a review of criminal justice policy which set out the Home Office's main 'preoccupations', the most challenging of these being to reduce both the size of the prison population and the proportionate use of custody by the courts. While this 'standstill' policy sought to hold the line on prison population size, it could not be said to amount to a concerted strategy to effect substantial reductions.[5] In stating that '(t)here is an inconsistency between the publicly avowed policy of using custody as a last resort for the really serious or dangerous offender and actual practice', the authors of the Review acknowledged the perennial and sensitive issues prompted by the minimal level of conversation between the Home Office and the judiciary.[6] Shortly after Margaret Thatcher won the 1979 General Election, the Crime Policy Planning Unit was abolished. Although the Home Office Research Unit in turn became the Research and Planning Unit, its task was more one of policy analysis, leaving strategic planning to those responsible within the ordinary structures of the Home Office. It was this chequered history of formalising the policy-making process which David Faulkner inherited in September 1982 when he assumed responsibility for criminal policy.

After reading classics at Oxford and completing his National Service, David Faulkner joined the Home Office in 1959 where he remained for most of his civil service career until early retirement in February 1992. Among various posts within the Home Office he was private secretary to the home secretary, James Callaghan, involved in plans, later aborted, to reform the House of Lords[7], and had a period in the Cabinet Office. Based in the prison department in the early 1970s, he was responsible for women's institutions and played a leading role in the redesign of Holloway prison, pointing Britain's largest women's establishment in a 'treatment' direction.[8] At this time he also was responsible for young offenders, with close involvement in the 'normalisation' of regimes through initiatives such as the development of 'neighbourhood borstals', as a means of linking these institutions to the wider community.[9]

David Faulkner's main influence on criminal policy dated from his appointment in September 1980 as director of operational policy within the prison department, and subsequently from September 1982 until October 1990, when as a deputy under-secretary he was responsible for the criminal, general and statistical departments and for the research and planning unit.[10] His specific responsibilities covered the probation service, sentencing including community penalties, research and statistics, and the scope of the criminal law. Although his formal jurisdiction did not extend to the police and prison services, or, for a while, to crime prevention issues, these boundaries did not restrict his vision of the total picture. Faulkner retained these responsibilities for a period which covered the last nine months of William Whitelaw's home secretaryship and continued throughout the tenures of both Leon Brittan and Douglas Hurd and during all but the last month of David Waddington's year at the Home Office. This was an unusually lengthy period of time for a senior official to remain at the same job. As Paul Rock has aptly noted, Faulkner 'became something of an authority in criminal justice matters, one of those unusual civil servants known and talked about by name. He was publicly associated with his accomplishments.'[11] Rock later added that Faulkner

> came to shed some of the anonymity and distance of his predecessors, not only initiating ventures but bringing them to a conclusion, and assuming (and being seen by others to assume) a clear personal authorship of specific policies. He was, in short, a highly placed and powerful man who

was bolder than most, more open and more candid, one who played an adventurous role within the rules.[12]

In the opinion of a former Home Office minister and later chairman of the Parole Board, Lord Windlesham, Faulkner's 'knowledge and experience of criminal policy, allied to the sophistication of his mind and methods, earned him an unsurpassed reputation inside and outside the public service.'[13]

Faulkner's general approach to criminal policy became evident when he returned to the Prison Department in September 1980 as director of operational policy. He sought to build bridges with academics, journalists and people in the voluntary sector including pressure groups such as the Howard League for Penal Reform and the National Association for the Care and Resettlement of Offenders (NACRO). These wider contacts served several purposes, not least being to work out what the notion of 'justice' might mean within the prison setting. It was typical of Faulkner, for example, to set up in July 1981 a small discussion group which, every other month or so, brought together at NACRO headquarters a handful of senior colleagues and academics. A somewhat similar group, reflecting his wider responsibilities, continued to meet under his auspices between 1982-90. These discussion groups consisted of a dozen or so people, meeting in the early evening over wine and sandwiches. Roy King, one of the participants in the first of these groups, has recalled that the meetings

> were confidential in the sense that no-one would have wished to embarrass another member of the group by repeating things better not said in public, but if the discussion stimulated ideas for an article or for an initiative within the Prison Department so much the better . . . Virtually no subject was excluded from the agenda of the meetings, and as the members of the group developed understanding and mutual respect so there was an unprecedented sharing of data and ideas, with opinions vigorously and freely expressed.[14]

In Windlesham's judgement, these informal meetings 'provided a sounding board, enabling the civil servants to keep abreast of the state of reformist opinion, and for the penal reform groups and academic researchers to obtain an insight into current thinking at the Home Office.'[15] Interviewed in 1990, Faulkner, himself, commented that the discussion group

> partly refreshes and partly it helps to inform what we do in the office . . . there are certainly colleagues in this building who would feel

uncomfortable in that sort of setting. It is I think a matter of temperament. Some colleagues feel comfortable and enjoy that sort of exchange. Others feel threatened by it, or for one reason or another uncomfortable. That is something you accept, but for those who feel comfortable in the setting, I think most of us found that it is at least fun, and often useful.[16]

Between 1980-83, Faulkner worked closely with William Whitelaw in a largely unsuccessful effort to place a ceiling on the size of the prison population.[17] Faulkner commented a few years later that, while Whitelaw might not have had a vision of very precise goals or objectives,

> he had a very clear sense of direction, which I think everyone working at the Home Office at that time appreciated. We had a sense of corporate commitment and the Office had a deep sense of loyalty to him. In some ways I think that what is happening now had its foundations at that time. It was very much Willie Whitelaw's hope that the Department would be able to get on better terms with the judiciary, and have an understanding between the different elements of the system, some sense of common objectives and some shared commitments to achieving them.[18]

During this period the Home Office was preoccupied with efforts to forestall crisis, but there was also an openness to problems, characterised by the phrase associated with Denis Trevelyan, the head of the prison department, that crowded and squalid prison conditions constituted an 'affront to a civilised society'.

While some preliminary work was done on minimum standards for prison regimes, most activity was directed at attempts to reduce the prison population. In what was a remarkable appeal to principle, William Whitelaw bluntly spelled out the problem in a speech to magistrates in February 1981.

> Hopes for a substantial reduction in the prison population must, in my view, rest primarily on a renewed commitment to avoiding custody wherever possible and, in cases where imprisonment is thought essential, a move towards shorter sentences for all except the violent offender. I must emphasise that the case for change in these directions does not rest solely on the crisis in the prison system, grave though it is. There are also important considerations of principle which reflect a significant shift in penological thinking over the last decade or so . . . It is, I think, common ground that a continued increase in the prison population could not be sustained. So on present trends, I should be obliged to consider what legislative measures could be taken.[19]

Whitelaw described his speech as marking a new way forward but, in the event, this search for a principled framework to guide the use of imprisonment was shortlived. A scheme to effect earlier release procedures and expected to reduce prison numbers by up to five thousand ran into fierce opposition, first from the judiciary and then among factions of the Conservative Party. In turn, this initiative contributed to a very rough ride for Whitlelaw at the Party Conference later that year. With Whitelaw publicly humiliated, the proposed scheme was shelved.

Shortly after William Whitelaw's retreat, the judiciary were reassured that the prison places they required would be provided.[20] The few liberalising successes were mostly initiatives taken outside the Home Office, notably by the Parliamentary All Party Penal Affairs Group in overcoming the Government's opposition to statutory criteria governing the custodial sentencing of offenders under the age of twenty-one.[21] David Faulkner took up his key policy-making job at the Home Office shortly after Parliament had enacted this legislation, and when the new sentencing provisions were brought into effect in May 1983 he was at the centre of preparations for the significant changes ahead.[22] At a conference on the Criminal Justice Act 1982, convened by the Home Office, Faulkner commented that the occasion, attended by practitioners working across the criminal justice process, was an innovation and that 'we should like to feel that the opportunity it provides for the judiciary and the magistracy, the probation and social services, and representatives of the police, prisons and education service to meet informally might stimulate more frequent contact and discussion.' He remarked that the Act fitted into a changing pattern of assumptions, beliefs and attitudes over the past twenty-five years by recognising that non-custodial penalties were less costly than custody and less likely to reinforce criminality. The increased use of custody with respect to young offenders over recent years reflected, at least in part, an inference by the courts that only custody could mark society's disapproval of the offence. The provisions of the legislation sought to change this. Faulkner declared: 'The Act recognises that custody has a place for young offenders - but it is a very limited place.' In subsequent years, the 1982 legislation was to be regularly cited by David Faulkner as Parliament's endorsement of the principle of minimum intervention in responding to young people in trouble, and the impact which this provision was to have on sentencing practice was to encourage the Home Office to explore its wider application in the criminal courts.

Whitelaw's tenure as home secretary never recovered from its battering from fellow Conservatives, and in his memoirs he acknowleged his disappointment in not having been able to achieve more. Noting that Douglas Hurd was at that time faced with an even larger prison population, he was saddend that 'all too many people in positions of authority have turned their backs on the prison problems and prefer to look the other way. They appear to neglect the important contribution of a sensible sentencing and prison policy.'[23] The period from Whitelaw's retreat in the autumn of 1981 until the end of 1986 epitomised the pragmatic character of criminal policy-making in post-war Britain. The approach of Whitelaw's successor, Leon Brittan, was essentially one of managing events, and during Douglas Hurd's first two years as home secretary, there were only a few signs of positive stirrings. Acknowledging in 1991 that the Home Office did not have a tradition of vision or radical reform, Faulkner observed that it 'has usually followed from behind, reacting and responding, but doing it in a way which has tried to keep up the momentum of progress and a consistent sense of direction . . . and for the most part avoiding the dangers of political over-reaction or short-term opportunism.'

Between 1981-90 David Faulkner delivered some one hundred and twenty speeches at seminars, meetings and conferences around the country. This remarkable output is unlikely to have been exceeded in terms of breadth or quantity by any other contemporary British senior civil servant. Most of Faulkner's speeches were public events, but there were a small number of gatherings where Chatham House rules applied (remarks not to be attributed without the speaker's consent). While these speeches reflected the evolving concerns of ministers, they must also be considered as a significant aspect of Faulkner's pro-active stance. Over the first two or three years, he averaged one speaking engagement a month, but by 1985 the pace of these engagements had doubled and during his final years he addressed three or more meetings each month.[24] Faulkner's regular speaking reflected a sustained effort to create a supportive network of criminal justice practitioners and other people with interests in this area.

Taken a step further in 1989, he initiated a series of Home Office 'special conferences', each bringing together twenty or so leading criminal justice practitioners, together with Home Office officials, at both regional and national levels.[25] He was usually out of London one day a week, and his open approach to the criminal justice environment enabled him to establish a diversity of contacts in addition to those arising from his accessibility at the Home Office. 'All of this is more than ever important', commented Faulkner, 'where we have to work by influence and persuasion rather than direct control.' Aware of the many influences which shape criminal policy, he remarked in a lecture to the Howard League for Penal Reform in April 1983, that while he was 'sometimes thought to be at the centre of events and to be possessed of great power and influence', he was 'actually very conscious of his distance from the places where the important action takes place and of the very real, and proper, limitations on the home secretary's powers in spite of the great things which may be expected of this office.' Describing the delicate balance in the respective roles of senior civil servants and their ministers, Paul Rock has noted,

> it is part of the bureaucratic art of persuasion that new ideas appear unfocused and unformed at first: they are *supposed* to be so until they receive political authority . . . Decisions must always seem to flow down from those who are accountable, not rise fully formed from obscure officials below.[26]

Anything but an obscure official, Faulkner kept a careful eye on the dynamic relationship between civil servants and their ministers. Talking to Home Office colleagues a year or so before he retired, he observed that their relationship with ministers was emphatically not one of passive obedience by officials.

> Most of us joined the civil service in the expectation that we would have the opportunity to serve the public in a more positive way by developing our own ideas (or just picking up the ideas of others); by arranging them in a coherent order; by carrying them into the decision-making process; and eventually, if we persuaded ministers that they were good ideas, by putting them into effect . . . It is our job to see that ministers have a choice of realistic and properly thought out options available to them, especially at the stage when a new policy is to be introduced. To do that we need to use our judgement and imagination, to create situations in which new ideas can emerge, to test those ideas in discussion with colleagues and professional contacts, and to subject them to research and statistical analysis, often at a stage well before the issue reaches the point of ministerial decision or engages ministers' serious attention. It is hard work - it needs space and skill, and it needs persistence and commitment. It involves a considerable degree of openness with those inside and outside the Office, and therefore a certain amount of risk and courage to face it.[27]

Speaking to a Top Management Course in January 1987, Faulkner remarked that

> of course ministers carry the ultimate political responsibility and have the final decision and of course we work within the framework of their political objectives and priorities and principles. The stimulus for a

particular piece of action will sometimes be theirs and it will sometimes be ours: the important thing is that we must both be fully committed to it. Similarly if there are obstacles they will sometimes be found by ministers or sometimes by ourselves. But we must jointly accept or overcome them. Failures of analysis, advice or execution are ours and not theirs; ministers are entitled to expect from us vision, imagination and argument as well as information and compliance; and if it succeeds it is our success as well as theirs, even if they take any public credit that may be going.

In one of his first speeches, Faulkner outlined several themes which he was to develop and refine over the next decade. Calling his speech 'Cooperation and Conflict in the Criminal Justice System', he explored the purposes and objectives arising from a 'systems perspective' which faced constituent agencies such as the police, prisons, courts and the probation service. Over the last twenty-five years the overriding concern had been prison overcrowding with the result that pragmatism ('patching and tinkering') often ruled over principle. The way forward, he suggested, included practical planning for the individual areas of criminal justice and assembling better information about crime, victims and the operation of criminal justice. He argued that the 'establishment' consensus on criminal policy was breaking down, and as a consequence attitudes were becoming increasingly polarised, 'with an increasing public emphasis on individual punishment on the one hand and greater professional emphasis on what might be called the social response to offending on the other.' Those who held the first view claimed that crime was an absolute evil and had to be condemned and eradicated without compromise by means of a 'war on crime'. This approach implied an indefinite expansion of the criminal justice system, apart perhaps from the probation service. By contrast, adherents of the contrary position supported efforts to reduce crime through all available methods of social intervention and application of wider policies within education, housing and social services, decriminalisation of certain offences, diversion of offenders at the pre-court stage, development of conciliation and compensation schemes between offenders and victims and closer links between prisoners and their communities.

Faulkner quite often made use of contrasting perspectives of this sort. Sometimes he highlighted the choice that had to be made; on other occasions, he observed that those who administer or work within the criminal justice arena had to try and reconcile contrasting points of view.[28] Regarding the dichotomy outlined in the previous paragraph, Faulkner's suggestion as to a way forward is instructive:

The policies through which this kind of reconciliation might be brought about include all the available methods of social intervention and the application of wider social policies in fields such as education, housing and social services; the development of schemes for compensation and conciliation between offenders and their victims and for victim support; measures designed to integrate those serving or having recently served sentences more closely into their own communities; the diversion of offenders from the criminal justice process, for example by cautioning or the application of non-criminal procedures; and the decriminalisation of certain offences, especially those which are of a regulatory nature and with which the courts might not have to be involved.

This early speech by Faulkner set the tone for much of what was to follow over the next eight years. It spanned the breadth of criminal policy, seeking to connect with broader aspects of social policy. He boldly articulated the policy choices, asserting that much depended upon the direction in which the criminal policy discourse moved forward. He also emphasised the care required in the choice of words and the tone used with regard to crime and offenders, insisting that 'the language of warfare is inappropriate and potentially dangerous.'

A year after Leon Brittan's arrival at the Home Office *Criminal Justice: A Working Paper* was published. Described as an 'operating manual' for practitioners, the intent was to clarify the objectives of criminal justice and to describe how the 'system' worked.[29] As one observer later noted, however, the main impression of the document was 'of a primary concern with practical details and the efficient management of the different parts of the criminal justice system'.[30] It seems likely that Faulkner was disappointed in the narrowness of this document, and he later remarked upon its traditionally pragmatic tone, noting that it neither addressed sentencing principles nor the purposes of custodial treatment. While the Working Paper insisted upon viewing criminal justice as a 'system', Faulkner was anxious to discourage simplistic ways of thinking about the diverse and complicated institutions of criminal justice, emphasising that the divisions between the different services had the purpose of protecting the individual and the suspect.

Faulkner's ability to handle the volatile political context of criminal policy-making was apparent in wide ranging remarks to a training seminar organized by the Judicial Studies Board in January 1985. He referred to public impatience with rising levels of recorded crime and to the victims' movement converging to create a political situation to which Leon Brittan had to respond firmly when he took office after the June 1983 election. For prisoners sentenced for violent or sexual offences, parole was to be sharply restricted, although the release of short-term prisoners was to be accelerated. The prison building programme was to be extended, along with an increase of maximum sentence for certain offences involving firearms, and there was to be a right of reference by the Attorney-General to the court of appeal with respect to 'unduly lenient' sentences.[31] After summarising these proposals, Faulkner remarked that the Home Office no longer claimed that measures taken within the criminal justice system were by themselves likely to have measurable effects on the general level of crime. This led him back to the themes of the Working Paper, including the balance between the rights of the individual and the community at large. He commented further that the package as a whole could be regarded as a balance between liberal and tough measures. The Police and Criminal Evidence Act 1984, for example, bestowed wider powers upon the police; but the same statute also contained new safeguards for the individual citizen. In a neat turn of phrase, Faulkner observed that the new statutory codes of police practice 'may come to be regarded as one of the significant elements in the de-Orwellisation of 1984'.

By this time, the Government's Financial Management Initiative was a crucial part of the environment of all public services, providing Faulkner with a convenient framework for raising questions about the effectiveness of the various criminal justice agencies. 'In the Home Office it is now clearly recognized that policy-making and resource management are a single process not separate activities.' He emphasised that within this context a more clearly defined set of practical objectives was required for the police and the probation services and, at least to some degree, for the courts. In July 1985, discussing the issue of delayed court hearings, he made it clear that it was right to argue that lack of resources should not influence a judicial decision. Nevertheless, such decisions should be taken within the context of a coherent set of principles which took account of the resources available and which sought to maximise the effectiveness with which they were used. 'Justice and administration cannot be regarded as separate - they are part of the same process.' Faulkner, however, was careful to avoid an open-ended endorsement of the management perspective, and quoted an academic at the London Business School to the effect that accountable management blocked off lateral vision. To which he added: 'Lateral vision may not be the current fashion but may become so for the 1990s.' In several talks, Faulkner returned to the interdependence of criminal justice agencies, regretting that there was still no great incentive for managers in any

94

service to take a wider view of the system as a whole. But he was alert to the need to preserve a 'lack of fit' across the criminal justice process, insisting upon the operational independence of chief officers and on the notion of judicial independence.

> These principles are still regarded as having great constitutional importance and as providing necessary safeguards for the citizen against future totalitarian government. They are not easy to reconcile with a whole-hearted commitment to strategic planning for the system as a whole or to the vigorous application by central government of financial indicators or controls.

Finally, Faulkner was always ready to remind his audiences of the relatively marginal role of criminal justice in dealing with crime. Speaking in 1990 as head of the United Kingdom Delegation to the United Nations Congress on the Prevention of Crime and the Treatment of Offenders, he said:

> Social order can sometimes, to a limited extent and for a limited period, be imposed by repressive legislation, intensive supervision or severe punishment. But success in tackling crime depends ultimately on mutual respect, consideration for others and shared standards and values. It depends on a sense of common humanity shared between those in positions of power and those in positions of relative disadvantage.

PRISONS AND SENTENCING

One of Faulkner's central concerns was to move away from the traditionally pragmatic approach to criminal policy and to sketch the outlines of a principled framework. As noted earlier, Home Office policy had been defined invariably in terms of prison crowding; and when courts were advised to take account of the desperate state of prisons in making decisions about custody at both the remand and sentencing stages, many judges and magistrates felt they were being urged to give priority to expediency for the convenience of central government. Fundamental issues such as the principles governing the removal of an individual's liberty were left unaddressed. Also arising from this tendency to pragmatism was a view of probation and community service orders as 'alternatives to custody' rather than as sentences in their own right. This perspective had reinforced the propensity of sentencers to start with custody in their minds and only thereafter to consider other dispositions.[32] In October 1987 Faulkner told an audience of magistrates that one of the tragedies of the previous twenty-five years was how prison overcrowding had dominated and distorted the argument about penal policy.

> The argument ought to have been on what scale, for what purpose and for what sort of offenders the ultimate sanction of imprisonment ought to be used. Instead it has been mostly about how we could reduce prison overcrowding and what sentencing and other devices could be introduced to achieve that result. The consequence has been that what ought to have been an argument of principle has become confused with arguments of expediency and cost, and the whole debate has become overlaid with cynical suspicion and unhealthy recriminations between the judiciary and the executive with the probation service placed awkwardly in the middle . . . I (would) prefer to begin by asking what place imprisonment has or ought to have in our arrangements for dealing with crime before asking how we might move it about in the sentencing structure.

On another occasion, commenting upon the tensions between the Home Office and the judiciary, Faulkner maintained that

> the fundamental reason is that the Home Office has a vested interest in reducing or keeping down the prison population, and any discussion of sentencing in which we argue for the development and greater use of non-custodial disposals tends to be tainted by the feeling that it's an argument of expediency designed to save the Government money on prison building.

Ironically, however, a principled and comprehensive approach would mean confronting the judiciary with the proposition that it was Parliament's task to create a more structured sentencing framework. But to embark down this road would be to trespass upon what the judges firmly regarded as their exclusive turf.[33] For Faulkner and his Home Office colleagues, memories were all too fresh of William Whitelaw's retreat in the face of the judiciary a few years earlier.

Much of what Faulkner had to say in the early 1980s about the place of prisons within the criminal justice process and the nature of prison regimes foreshadowed to a remarkable degree the reform agenda adopted by Lord Justice Woolf's enquiry in the wake of the large scale prison disturbances of April 1990.[34] Addressing the Parole Board in February 1983, Faulkner emphasised that the prison system had to be be located within the context of the overall purposes of the criminal justice system. The police and probation services were rethinking their objectives, and so should be the prison service. It had been difficult, he found, to engage in discussions with the prison service about the merits of a justice model, but he endorsed Lord Wilberforce's proposition, namely that: 'Under English law, a convicted prisoner in spite of his imprisonment, retains all civil rights which are not taken away expressly or by necessary implication.'[35] For Faulkner, this was the starting point for thinking about the code of minimum standards then being developed within the Prison Department.[36] He insisted that 'a prison should be a civilized community in which prisoners and staff can live and work together as decent human beings.' Similarly, in August 1986 in summarising a conference held at the Prison Service College, he wrote that

> as discussion progressed it became clear that the Prison Service had important opportunities for constructive action in the design of regimes and the construction of a "throughcare" programme which would be relevant to the urban communities from which most prisoners came and to which they would return. The geographical isolation of many establishments, the pressure of overcrowding and the resulting distribution of the population and problems over resources were obvious inhibiting factors. Even so, professionalism in the treatment of individuals and relations between staff and inmates to preserve hope, self respect and confidence; the explicit recognition of an inmate's interest and association with the community from which he came and to which he would return; and the provision of opportunities to support and foster that association . . . were all matters to which the prison service would like to devote increasing attention.

With Douglas Hurd, who replaced Leon Brittan as home secretary in September 1985, came a calmer pair of hands. Initially, the policy agenda retained a focus on attempting to align prison numbers and resources. This was reflected in Faulkner's remarks to probation officers in March 1986 in which he emphasised the government's priorities to strengthen the police and expand the prison system.

> The prison building programme is designed to improve the conditions in local prisons against the recognition that in present circumstances there would be virtually no public support for the alternative solution of a substantial reduction in the prison population or for that matter any politically acceptable means of achieving that result.

But Faulkner also wove into this speech the striking observation that despite an increased use by the courts of probation, disappointment remained that the proportionate use of custody had increased from 14.1% to 16.4% between 1979-1984. He went on to say that (t)he task for the next few years must be to try and increase the market share of probation and community service by increasing the numbers of such orders by, say, five percent a year and doing so in the profitable sector of the market which is at present held by custody . . . I still hope that statements of local objectives and priorities will include some target figures - both for the total number of orders you want to make and for the type of case to which you want to give priority.

For a senior civil servant to publicly propose a precise reductionist target of this sort was highly unusual. This speech hinted at a marked departure from the 'standstill' pragmatism which had so dominated criminal policy over the previous two decades.

In September 1986, and with the number of people in prison still rapidly climbing, Faulkner clearly articulated the pending policy dilemma. Seemingly anticipating issues to be directly confronted a year hence, he observed that

the question for the next few years is whether we are going to see a continuing rise in the prison population which will eventually cancel the intended benefits of the prison building programme. Whether the Government will commit itself to an even greater investment in prison building or whether it is possible to stabilise our use of imprisonment around the present level, I would like to think that the time has come for a judgement which the judiciary and the executive will in some way be able to make together.

He did not shirk from countering the championship of imprisonment that was so evident across the Atlantic. Speaking to the Magistrates' Association in Swansea, he cautioned his audience to be wary of comparisons with the United States that might be presented as an example of a sentencing practice to be emulated, and questioned the analysis of prison and crime data in the United States, maintaining that the claims being made by 'Republican Party politicians' for the incapacitative effects of imprisonment upon the level of crime were misplaced.[37]

The pace of events was now gathering pace, and in January 1987 Faulkner shared some prescient thoughts with a Top Management Seminar:

At less frequent intervals we have the opportunity of a more radical and longer term review of what we are doing by the need to brief an incoming home secretary, especially, but not only, after a General Election. Our experience over the years has been that changes in personality can be just as significant as changes of political administration.

With Mrs Thatcher's third election victory in June 1987, it was a more confident Douglas Hurd that returned to the Home Office. Hurd had played a key role in drafting the Conservative Party manifesto which had taken an unusually broad view of crime and criminal policy. It stated, for example, that the government was providing 'a tough legal framework for sentencing; by building the prisons in which to take those who pose a threat to society - and by keeping out of prison those who do not . . . '[38] Faulkner later commented that

> (t)he lesson of the last twenty years is that the problem of crime cannot be solved by the criminal justice system alone. Other measures are needed to reduce crime and fear of crime and the Conservative Party Manifesto recognises that government alone cannot tackle such deep-rooted problems easily or quickly.

Lord Windlesham has noted that 'Hurd sensed that the time was ripe to draw together several strands of policy, weaving them together into a coherent pattern and projecting them as a whole.'[39] A seminar held at Leeds Castle in Kent on 28 September 1987 was very much Douglas Hurd's idea. The importance of this Home Office 'away day', attended by the complete team of Home Office ministers and key officials, was that it reinforced the transformation of criminal policy which was already underway. Reflecting Hurd's 'one nation' Toryism, the seminar addressed crime prevention, sentencing and the future of the probation service, and Windlesham, who has provided the fullest published account, noted that it 'soon came to be recognised as a milestone in the development of policies that had been consciously designed as part of a system of criminal justice, rather than a random collection of timely proposals for change.'[40]

With the home secretary in the chair and officials looking on, the responsible junior ministers gave the initial presentations. John Patten, who had joined the Home Office in June with a broad criminal policy brief, opened, curiously, with an expansionist recipe. But in sharp contrast, Lord Caithness, who was responsible for the prison system, used carefully prepared charts to make it clear that if current prison population trends were allowed to continue, an ammesty of prisoners might be inevitable. This was totally unacceptable to Hurd, who had ruled out such a step two months earlier. By the end of the discussion, ministers agreed that a reductionist course had to be found. John Patten, as Windlesham has noted, was soon 'firmly established as the home secretary's lieutenant on all matters concerning criminal policy' and became an enthusiastic supporter of the reductionist way forward.[41] Speaking to magistrates a few weeks later Faulkner's remarks perhaps echoed his advice to ministers at Leeds Castle.

During the 1970s we succeeded in keeping the rate of increase in the prison population below the rate of increase in recorded crime. But we still make more use of imprisonment than almost any other country in Western Europe, and we know the prison population has surged, during the last three years, ahead of the increase in recorded crime, in spite of the extension in eligibility for parole under the Criminal Justice Act 1982 and the increase in remission to 50% for sentences of under 12 months which came into effect in August. The prospect is one of a continuing rise in the prison population and a continuing problem of overcrowding despite the massive and hugely expensive programme of prison building which is now in progress. This is a dangerous and damaging situation, not only for the prison service but also for the courts, the public and the quality of justice.

He went on to outline what was to emerge as the philosophical core of the 1990 white paper and subsequent Criminal Justice Act 1991 with an exploration of sentencing rationales in which he particularly focused upon 'just deserts'. While the notion of 'just deserts' was first articulated by liberal academics in the United States in the mid 1970s,[42] it seems likely that Faulkner was influenced primarily by the writings of the British legal scholar, Andrew Ashworth, who had argued that 'the most urgent question is the effect of a previous criminal record. What approach should be taken to the sentencing of persistent offenders? I suggest we should consider moving towards a more rigorous principle . . . so that an offender who commits a modest theft for the fifth . . . or fifteenth time should not be at risk of a custodial sentence.'[43] Faulkner acknowledged that

at one time many of us would have thought "just deserts" to be an unacceptably illiberal principle. But I am afraid that in recent years more injustice has been done in the name of treatment, training and rehabilitation than it has ever been in the name of retribution, and in the present state of knowledge I find myself more attracted to the relatively straightforward and unambiguous principle of retribution than to the contortions and compromises involved in other approaches.

In this groundbreaking speech, Faulkner went on to say that in proposing a retributive view of sentencing he was

not of course suggesting that sentencing should take place in isolation from what the country or community is trying to do about crime. Two lines of argument are particularly significant in this respect. One is the importance of a collective, community-based approach in which the community as a whole accepts some responsibility for offending behaviour and is prepared to do something about it and about the offenders and potential offenders who are in its midst. It should not regard offenders and potential offenders as being some kind of external threat, as people who are different from ourselves and who do not properly belong in our own society and against whom we need to raise physical defences or who ought to be contained in their ghettos or failing that in prison.

The court's sentence should not increase the propensity of the offender to commit further offences and it should reinforce or leave intact such positive influences or opportunities that might be available, to which he added that

all the evidence shows that custody is not only your most severe and ultimate punishment but also one most likely to be followed by further offending . . . is most disabling in removing him from the influences and opportunities which may be of a lasting benefit, however hard the prison service may try to provide substitutes within the prison regime.

This was a most remarkable speech, reflecting the extent to which thinking within the higher reaches of the Home Office had advanced by this time. It marked the first full public airing of ideas that would form the basis of the government's policy proposals to be set out in the green and white papers still, respectively, eight and twenty-two months away. Faulkner's speeches over the next few months anticipated the green paper's key themes. In November 1987 he told a conference that 'we must tackle crime and fear of crime before we can expect to see a reduction in prison overcrowding through less severe sentencing reflecting a more tolerant public attitude.' The main target group was to be young adult offenders, and he urged that practice build upon the successful work with juveniles which had demonstrated that 'custody can be avoided without placing the public at risk of a higher incidence of crime.' He went on to say that 'we might eventually see the end of custody for those of school age, except perhaps under section 53 of the Children and Young Persons Act 1933, or an extension of the jurisdiction of the juvenile court to include seventeen-year-olds or even beyond.'

The green paper, published in June 1988, stated that imprisonment limited the offender's personal responsibility for taking everyday decisions; restricted individual initiative and freedom of choice; and diminished the offender's sense of responsibility and self-reliance. It went on to ask whether too many people were being sent to prison and whether the public could more effectively be protected from recidivist burglars and thieves by other means.[44] It proceeded to set forth ideas about how the notion of 'punishment in the community' might be operationalised. With the green paper in the public domain, Faulkner stressed that it was part of a much wider programme which also addressed crime prevention and provision for victims. He argued that 'custody is not effective as a means of reducing crime. Apart from its high cost, which even sentencers ought to take into account, it had a criminalising effect especially on young people.' He went on to tell his NACRO audience that '(custody) reinforces crime and criminality rather than reducing it . . . it cannot be right to regard custody as the normal or standard response to crime. The green paper takes as its starting point the need to find other means of dealing with the problems it creates.' However, it was not primarily about reducing overcrowding but rather about reducing crime, especially that committed by young adults. For this to be achieved, there needed to be a more coherent, self-confident and self-reliant community. He hoped that the green paper's approach might lead to the diversion of three thousand young adults from custodial sentences.[45]

By this time, Faulkner was arguing that the principle of minimum intervention should be regarded as central to sentencing practice. Speaking to JUSTICE in February 1989, he proposed that

> minimum intervention should be the guiding principle for all sentences, but that it needs to be applied consistently with the requirements of deterrence, protection of the public and denunciation and retribution; in other words a sentence in a particular case should be the lowest possible that will not be seen as encouraging future offending, placing the public at risk or condoning the crime that has been committed.

After drawing attention to a statement by the home secretary the previous year on prison overcrowding, he reviewed various means of influencing sentencing practice, including legislation to increase or reduce maxima and the specification of sentencing criteria. But he then made the highly significant observation that it was local consultation and practice that held out the greatest promise for change.

> This, rather than any new legislation or initiative from the Court of Appeal, is what brought about the dramatic change in sentencing for juveniles, and it is the initiative of local practitioners that has made West Germany one of the very few West European countries to have reduced its prison population within the last few years.[46] It is where the hopes for the

green paper have been based, but it requires a degree of local cooperation and understanding which may be difficult to achieve.

As he pointed out on another occasion,

the proposals in the green paper start from the successful experience with juveniles, and the lack of evidence that an increase in the use of community sentences would lead to an increase in crime, or put the public at risk. Given the criminalizing effect of custody, and some research evidence, it is likely to have the opposite effect. Community sentences would enable offenders to remain in the community, learning to cope with the problems, pressures and responsibilities which surround them, and gaining self-reliance and self-discipline. Custody absolves them from all of these and is the ultimate form of the "dependency culture".[47]

Faulkner was not reticent in sharply underlining the government's point of departure on criminal policy.

The green paper marked a significant change in the direction of Home Office and government thinking . . . The starting point is that for the middle range of offenders - not the most serious or most dangerous but including persistent thieves and non-domestic burglars - there has to be a better way of dealing with their offenses , a better form of punishment than custody.

In this speech to a conference on young offenders, Faulkner went on to say that

whether it succeeds depends on whether we can construct programmes which have a demonstrable and, if possible, measurable effect on offending behaviour, and on whether they can also be regarded as sufficiently tough and demanding to satisfy the courts and the wider public that they are an adequate punishment.

Mr Hurd had used the opportunity of the 1989 Conservative Party conference to make clear his own commitment to the new approach by telling delegates:

The guiding principle is that every convicted criminal should receive his just deserts . . . But prison should not be the only rigorous punishment. Take the teenage thief, for example. We can put him idling in a prison cell, at huge expense to the taxpayer, learning probably new tricks from old lags. Or, I think better, we can put him to something useful: scrubbing the graffiti off the walls; cleaning up the litter in his neighbourhood. The most important is still to come: keeping his job, working for his living, but with deductions so that he pays compensation to his victim. So the courts need, and will have, a wider and tougher range of these community-based punishments.[48]

Talking to magistrates a few weeks later, Faulkner drew attention to this endorsement by the home secretary of 'just deserts', adding that it certainly did not follow that the sentence imposed on a persistent offender had to be custody.

Once the green paper had been published, ministers were determined to make every effort to obtain the support of the judiciary. Summarising a meeting of deputy chief probation officers four months later, Faulkner noted that among those present there remained continuing uncertainty about the attitude of judges. 'The sentencing practice of the higher judiciary may also need changing in the light of the green paper. There was a feeling that different parts of the system had received different messages.' The awkward problem had resurfaced of finding a satisfactory means of consultation so as to avoid a breakdown of relations between the Home Office and the judiciary. It was decided that the first step should be a high-level meeting in conditions of complete privacy. This took the form of a two-day conference at Ditchley Park House in September 1989 to which the Lord Chief Justice and other senior practitioners were invited for a preview and discussion of the main themes of the forthcoming legislative proposals. This gathering at the most senior level was in due course to be complemented by the extensive programme of Home Office 'special conferences'.[49] But within a month or so of the Ditchley Park meeting, Mr Hurd was abruptly transplanted to the Foreign Office, leaving the white paper in its final drafting stage.

The new home secretary was David Waddington who had been Leader of the House of Commons. Although he was widely regarded as a hard-liner, as evidenced by his support for the restoration of capital punishment, Waddington stood by the essence of the white paper. In one section, which was to become widely quoted, the white paper stated that

> however much prison staff try to inject a positive purpose into the regime, as they do, prison is a society which requires virtually no sense of personal responsibility from prisoners. Normal social or working habits do not fit. The opportunity to learn from other prisoners is pervasive. For most offenders, imprisonment has to be justified in terms of public protection, denunciation and retribution. Otherwise it can be an expensive way of making bad people worse. The prospects of reforming offenders are

usually much better if they stay in the community, provided the public is properly protected.[50]

However, Waddington insisted that incapacitative sentences (extending beyond what was required by desert but limited by the maximum penalty) be allowable for the more serious violent and sexual offenders.[51] This demand by the new home secretary represented a significant departure from the way that 'just deserts' had been viewed by Faulkner and his colleagues, but it was perhaps regarded as essential to securing passage of the bill. On the other hand, Waddington announced in September 1990, at the annual conference of the Howard League for Penal Reform, that fourteen-year-olds would no longer be eligible for custodial sentences.

Mr Waddington's announcement must have given considerable satisfaction to Faulkner, but by this time his period of pivotal influence was drawing to a close. In June 1990, in one of his last speeches before being moved sideways to another post in the Home Office, he referred to the decisions which had been taken at Leeds Castle three years earlier. 'That was when Ministers decided that there must be a better way to deal with crime than by locking people up on the present scale.' In a keynote address to the Institute for the Study and Treatment of Delinquency, Faulkner warned that drafting the forthcoming bill would be an important and difficult exercise. He foresaw what was to become the most contentious part of the legislation, remarking that 'aspects of the drafting where special care is needed include the treatment of persistent and multiple offences.' He was 'cautiously optimistic' that judges would reduce sentence lengths in line with the proposals of a committee chaired by Lord Carlisle on the parole system.[52] The crucial issue was judicial confidence in the probation service and developments across the criminal justice process. But there was also the wider public and political context, and he acknowledged that 'it is a remarkable political achievement to have brought proposals of this kind to a stage of broad political consensus in the way that it has been done over the last three years.' He warned, however, that continued political support could not be taken for granted especially if the rising trend in reported crime were to re-assert itself. He emphasised that the white paper's approach relied upon a combination of legislation, judicial guidance and effective management; but it also depended upon the personal enthusiasm of many thousands of individuals in different services and professions. His concluding note was that 'the proposals in the white paper are primarily about finding a better way to tackle crime and about better standards of justice and its administration. We hope that they will incidentally reduce the prison population.'

YOUNG OFFENDERS

The first Thatcher government had announced that it would revive the 'short, sharp shock' in detention centre regimes for young offenders. In the event, William Whitelaw proceeded with an experiment involving random allocation to two 'tough' institutions and two regular detention centres. A long drawn-out study by prison department psychologists was published eventually in the summer of 1984. To the disappointment of ministers, the study found that the stricter regimes were not associated with lower rates of recidivism. Speaking to the Magistrates' Association shortly after the findings were made public, Faulkner contended that the data did not support the view that the early use of custody had a salutary effect. He pointed out that sentencing trends suggested an increasing punitiveness between 1968-1982, with juveniles more severely dealt with than their adult counterparts. Asking what lay behind this trend, he drew attention to geographical disparities and urged magistrates to ensure that clerks recorded figures so that comparisons might be made across courts and over time. Although he made no specific reference to the detention centre study, it must have been very much on the minds of his audience, given Leon Brittan's strong support for tougher detention centre regimes. Indeed it was the determined resolve by magistrates over the next few years to avoid making detention centre orders that led to the eventual demise of this sanction in the Criminal Justice Act 1988.

It had become evident as early as 1983 that the practice of both the police and courts in dealing with juvenile offenders was changing. An increasing proportion of juveniles were being formally cautioned by the police, and juvenile court (as it was then known) caseloads were falling sharply. Equally striking was the tendency on the part of the courts to use custodial sentences with lessening frequency. This de-escalatory change of practice marked a powerful anti-custody ethos on the part of many of practice combined with close collaboration by agencies at the local level.[53] This turning of the tide of opinion among magistrates and other practitioners began while Leon Brittan was still the home secretary. In fact, six months before Brittan's departure, Faulkner was explicitly endorsing the principle of minimum intervention, stressing 'the ordinary natural forces of the family and society should be allowed to work and be reinforced for as long as possible . . . I hope the principle of minimum intervention is now well understood and widely accepted.' A year or so later, and with Douglas Hurd as home secretary, Faulkner told a meeting of the Magistrates' Association that juvenile crime, unlike crime generally, was not increasing. To a similar audience he pointed out that 'the great majority of young people grow out of crime successfully and become law abiding citizens; but the greater the degree of the offender's involvement with the criminal justice system and the greater the extent of its intervention in his or her life, the more likely he or she is to continue offending.' He again stressed that 'the principle I would like to suggest for juvenile justice is therefore one of "minimum intervention". It was not, I think, expressed in this way during the passage of the 1982 Criminal Justice Act but it is a theme which runs through all its juvenile justice provisions.' In March 1987, after commenting that juvenile crime was falling, he again referred magistrates to Mr Hurd.

> The principle that the Home Secretary has himself supported in juvenile sentencing is one of minimum intervention and of leaving the high intervention disposals for as long as you can. The French take it for granted that keeping youngsters out of custody is one way to reduce crime, and the courts like Basingstoke and Northampton which have virtually stopped using custody for juveniles have found that juvenile offending has in fact decreased.[54]

Faulkner was quick to recognise that this pattern of effective juvenile justice practice might shape not only policy regarding young offenders but also could be more generally applied to criminal policy. The key was to develop and exploit positive opportunities and influences in the community.

THE CHANGING ROLE OF THE PROBATION SERVICE

The probation service remained a central preoccupation for David Faulkner. Unlike prisons and the courts, the local area probation services in England and Wales fell directly within his area of responsibilities, and he recognised at once that these were critical to the required transformation of policy. The probation service was crucial in any move toward tackling crime in the community rather than investing more resources within prisons. This meant, as Faulkner stated in July 1989, that 'the transformation from a social work agency to a criminal justice agency with a social work base must be completed if the service is to do what is now expected of it.' The task was one that required considerable diplomacy. Faulkner and his colleagues in the probation division of the Home Office were the point of contact between practitioners and ministers, among whom there existed considerable mutual suspicion. In directing his attention to the probation service, Faulkner insisted that 'community penalties' acquire a new public image. The supervision experience should be demanding and be backed by the courts in dealing with breaches of the order's requirements. But care also had to be taken not to overplay this theme, and Faulkner was anxious that sight not be lost of the service's traditional values which embraced a humanitarian offer of help and advice, refined over the years by professional social work training. The immense difficulties of achieving a balanced way forward were all too apparent, as evidenced in his frequent speeches to meetings of probation officers.

In May 1984, a national statement on objectives and priorities for the probation service was published, with the expectation that it be applied in terms of local probation area plans.[55] Faulkner stressed to his probation audiences that there was a problem of confidence between them and the Crown Courts which had to be acknowledged. It was very much about what the probation service actually offered the courts and the way in which it was offered. He warned that if the probation service is 'thought feeble and disorganized it will have very little influence at all.' His audience was reminded that although there had been a sixty percent increase in real terms in spending on the probation service since 1979/80, representing the fastest rate of growth of any criminal justice agency, there had been a danger that the probation service, in the harsher circumstances of the time, might have lost its influence and slipped gradually into a position of insignificance. This has not happened but it was vital to maintain the momentum.

Speaking on the future of the probation service at the annual conference of the National Association of Probation Officers in March 1986, he acknowledged that many probation officers felt uncertain about where the service was heading. 'I know that probation officers find it difficult and some of you may think it objectionable to attach priorities to your work. You may feel you are betraying your client but it must be done.' Faulkner was explicit about the green paper's implications for the probation service, commenting that its proposals were based upon 'the belief, supported by research and experience with juveniles, but still needing to be demonstrated by the probation service's own performance that crime can be reduced more effectively by community-based measures than by custody and this applies especially to young people.' It was therefore necessary for the probation service to acknowledge its control function as part of its professionalism and its public profile.

> This is generally accepted, at least by probation management. But the service also has to come to terms with the notion of punishment . . . their acknowledgement of control and punishment in the community is not in any sense a betrayal of the service's own traditions and values. It is rather a recognition of the service's own traditions and values, and an endorsement of the service's own view that respect for the individual, a sense of personal identity and autonomy, and self-discipline and self-control are a better foundation on which to reduce offending than the disabling and often humiliating experience of imprisonment.

This theme was articulated with particular clarity in a speech, widely circulated, to the Clarke Hall Conference in July 1989. Social work values had their place but he hoped this did not mean an exclusive commitment to the interests of the so-called client.[56] While he believed that the probation service was now largely reconciled to issues of control, as far as punishment was concerned, 'there (were) still some problems.'

The message for the probation service which Faulkner repeated at meetings all over the country was that the probation service had to be both willing and equipped to take on a more significant role within the criminal justice process. If this was to happen, it would be necessary for the work of probation officers to be understood in terms of 'punishment in the community'. A change was required in language and also in the attitudes of probation service personnel. But the strategy implicit in the green paper had been sharply criticised not only in some probation service circles but also among academics. For example, at a seminar organized by the London School of Economics in April 1989, David Garland of Edinburgh University stated that the problem with the green paper

> is that for all its progressive suggestions it tends to reinforce the punitive elements of our culture. It underlies the current sentencing pattern, but it refuses to challenge or even question this culture of severity . . . (I)t seems altogether unreasonable to demand that probation workers adapt themselves to fit a punitive mentality which itself remains beyond criticism.[57]

Faulkner's response was swift.

Punishment in the community has been criticised as likely to reinforce society's instincts for repression and rejection, and I share the implied concern that we must not create an isolated, criminalized and potentially hostile underclass . . . if properly applied, the notion of punishment in the community should help to reinforce the community's sense of responsibility for its misfits and failures.

He was convinced that the probation service did have to move some way towards the government's view of its role if it were to assume the 'centre stage' position which was envisaged.

CRIME PREVENTION

A working group on crime prevention had been set up in 1975, and a crime prevention unit established within the police department of the Home Office eight years later. Faulkner identified 1982 as the year when crime prevention began to be seen as a serious subject, commenting that before then it 'was of very marginal interest for both central Government and the police. It was of no interest at all to the other criminal justice services, still less to local government or to other central government departments.' At a Home Office seminar attended by the police, local authorities and NACRO in the autumn of 1982, (Faulkner had just taken up his new position) the themes of inter-agency collaboration and community development emerged. It was this broader perception of crime prevention that was to be addressed in a Home Office circular which was signed by the permanent secretaries of five departments. The weaknesses of the circular, Faulkner later noted, were that 'no-one had overall responsibility for delivering crime prevention on the ground.'[58]

Faulkner recognised from the beginning that a coherent approach to criminal policy required the integration of crime prevention with issues of criminal justice. As he said in a speech in March 1985, 'there is an obvious and important link between preventive programmes in the community and court disposals for those who have committed offences and whom the court does not want to offend again.' Any progress on the crime prevention front relieved the unrealistic notions that criminal justice held the answers to concerns about crime. The issue of crime prevention, however, presented Faulkner with some immediate difficulties. Formal responsibility for crime prevention remained within the police department, and, for a while, his only direct route was through the research and planning unit. The Home

110

Office's research on crime prevention, which had commenced in the mid-1970s, was mostly directed at reducing the opportunities for at least certain types of crime to occur.[59] Over the next decade, however, the emphasis moved from 'situational' crime prevention towards the dynamics of particular communities in the generation and reduction of crime. In the first of many talks he was to give at judicial studies seminars, Faulkner described how policy was moving beyond 'locks, bolts and bars' into a more broadly based programme which included situational and environmental factors such as the design and management of housing estates, the provision and organization of local services and preventative work among people, especially young people, at risk. 'Community crime prevention (then) is not all of a piece . . . communities differ not only in character but also in the form in which crime affects them: some communities experience crime predominantly as victims: others also have members who themselves become involved in crime.' This much broader perspective on crime prevention and its part within criminal policy was to be the theme of an international conference convened in 1986 by the Home Office Research and Planning Unit.[60]

A further obstacle to substantive progress on crime prevention in Britain was the highly suspicious view of local authorities held by the Government. As one political commentator has put it: 'The validity of local government as a function relevant to British democracy ceased to be taken for granted. Wave upon wave of assaults on the financial independence of local authorities weakened their powers and cast doubt on their point.'[61] But it remained Faulkner's view that crime prevention was the sensible lead responsibility of local government.[62] As he remarked to a probation audience in May 1987: 'Success demands local energy and local commitment which are not often created spontaneously and not easy to generate. The local authority is the natural source of leadership but not all local authorities are able or perhaps willing to provide it.' Approaching the politically delicate issue of what role local government should play in the delivery of crime prevention, Faulkner's notes on a seminar of prison, police and probation officials, held in August 1986, revealed the participants' agreement that 'local authorities and, in particular, chief executives would have a crucial part to play in any developments of this kind' (for example, carrying forward the joint departmental circular).

In this country, central government's relations with local government are complicated at present . . . but despite the complications the chief executive looks as if he is the best agent we can find for this kind of purpose. But how do we engage his interest?

111

A month after the election of June 1987, in a key speech at the National Police College, Bramshill, Faulkner observed that over the previous three years a good basis of experience in crime prevention measures had been developed. 'The task is now to consolidate that experience and move on to the human and social side of crime prevention - to tackle some of the conditions which are conducive to offending and to try to strengthen and develop the more positive influences which can help to prevent it.' He linked this with young people on the margins of society, commenting that 'those who do not fit are easily rejected and we all know how easily rejection can lead to apathy and then to offending.' He explored the implications of this for the various criminal justice services and went on to make the link between crime prevention and sentencing.

> For the courts there is the lesson that there is nothing so disabling as custody and there is increasing evidence that diverting young people from custody may be one of the most effective crime prevention measures of all. A programme of this kind needs to be assembled and delivered at a local level and that is a task for the local authority. The police are, of course, involved throughout.

For Faulkner, the French experience of *politique de prevention* illustrated the integrated model which he had in mind. Talking to a probation audience in the spring of 1987 he described developments in France as representing 'a comprehensive approach to crime and social disorder which recognises the linkages between poor housing, bad schools, unemployment, racial tensions and a decaying physical environment and which tries to construct an integrated programme stimulated from the centre but delivered at the local level.' Eighteen months later, in the opening address to a conference on crime in Europe, he again drew attention to 'the French ideas of an integrated locally based approach, coordinated and stimulated from the centre, and of keeping a sensitive balance between the repressive and preventive approach to crime.' He added that these ideas were ones which 'we respect and have been pleased to apply in this country.'[63]

A further obstacle in approaching rational crime prevention policy arose from the barriers in effectively engaging with other central government departments such as housing, employment and education. As Windlesham has noted, some of the ideas which Faulkner and his colleagues had developed just prior to the Leeds Castle seminar under the heading 'Action for Youth' came to very little due to a lack of interdepartmental commitment.[64] But Faulkner was not deterred from addressing questions which are prompted by any serious consideration of crime prevention. In January 1987 at a Top Management Programme seminar (involving senior civil servants and senior executives from the private sector) he asked what were the possibilities and limits for Home Office intervention in broader issues of social policy?

> How as officials do we engage with the obvious political aspects? There is no point in Home Office officials trying to resist the expansion of private ownership of housing, the withdrawal of board and lodging allowance from young people who can perfectly well live at home . . . Nor is there any clearly established Home Office basis on which to do so. But there is an argument for saying that none of these things should be done in ways which leave an isolated minority of deserted or battered wives, young children and "difficult" young people living in crime ridden ghettos where they are even more deprived and vulnerable than they were before. How do we justify that kind of message? How do we get it across? How do we develop programmes to do something about it? And will it affect crime if we do? Getting answers to these questions is one of my New Year Resolutions and any help would be much appreciated.

He went even further down this uncharted road at a conference on 'surviving poverty', five months before he was moved away from criminal policy. He told participants at the conference jointly organized by NACRO and the Association of Chief Officers of Probation that the green and white papers meant that probation officers would, if anything, be more concerned to deal systematically with problems of poverty and to help offenders survive them than they had in the past. 'The integration between benefits policy and criminal justice policy has got to be got right.' Faulkner acknowledged the political sensitivities embodied in these issues, and, having outlined the government's rationale, he went on to tease out what might be done. This speech provided a particularly good example of Faulkner operating to the full in a public setting and within the constraints inherent in his status as a civil servant.

VICTIMS

Issues concerning the victims of crime did not receive a high profile in Faulkner's speeches. In his talks to organizations such as Victim Support he took a rather cautious line as to where issues of victims fitted within an overall scheme of criminal policy, largely because ministers were hesitant about deciding to fund victim support groups.

113

He stressed that offenders and their victims were very often the same sort of people, and he also acknowledged the dangers of victims being exploited for political purposes. He had found himself rather isolated at the United Nations Congress on Crime in 1985 when he expressed caution about the notion of 'victims' rights'. Paul Rock, in his definitive account of the Home Office and victim support groups, has noted that '(v)ictims remained diffracted and fragmented, an ad hoc collection of separate practices and images called criminal injuries compensation, victim support, crime surveys, compensation orders, and reparation.'[65] Rock has convincingly argued that victims of crime remained marginal and incidental to the pull of penal reform.[66]

RACE AND GENDER

Faulkner displayed neither hesitation nor temerity in addressing directly issues of discrimination within the context of criminal justice. He commented that 'all my experience has shown that race issues - and issues of gender - have to be treated as an integral part of policy formation and policy analysis, and as an integral part of management.' He was immediately impressed by the dearth of information and lack of routine monitoring. He was especially hard-hitting in remarks to probation audiences about ethnic monitoring, commenting on one occasion that 'the probation service seems to be deeply ambivalent about the whole issue.' In March 1985, the National Association of Probation Officers had voted to boycott efforts by the Home Office to introduce ethnic monitoring procedures. Two months later he told a conference of probation officers that they needed to face penetrating and difficult questions, and suggested to them that the police and prison service had a better story to tell. Further critical remarks followed on training and recruitment and he emphasised that monitoring also addressed management structures (and here, he suggested, the prison department provided a useful model). He made his position crystal clear in March 1986 at the annual conference of the National Association of Probation Officers: 'I do not see how a probation service can do its duty by the ethnic minorities without a system of ethnic monitoring . . . I hope that we can have a national system at least under test by the end of the year.'

Faulkner did not confine his concerns about race to members of the probation service. Speaking to the Magistrates' Association in April 1986, he remarked: 'Some of us think that there is a strong case for special training, but whether you have training or not, you need to be

The next step was obtaining the resources, and calculations were complicated by the fact that the prison population had already fallen quite substantially from its record level in the Spring of 1987. Faulkner concluded by describing the existing situation as being precarious, remarking that:

Some commentators are beginning to claim, without any real evidence, that the increase in recorded crime is because not enough people are being locked up. The reasons and the facts themselves are, of course, a good deal more complex, but the danger of a punitive reaction, especially as we approach another general election is a factor which has to be taken seriously into account.

ENDNOTES

1. Michael Moriarty, 'The policy-making process: how it is seen from the Home Office' in Nigel Walker (ed), *Penal Policy-Making in England* (Cambridge, Institute of Criminology, 1977), 134.

2. Anthony E Bottoms and Simon Stevenson, 'What Went Wrong?: Criminal Justice Policy in England and Wales, 1945-70', in David Downes (ed), *Unravelling Criminal Justice. Eleven British Studies* (London, Macmillan, 1992), 6; see also, Leon Radzinowicz, *Ideology and Crime. A study of Crime and its Social and Historical Context* (London, Heinemann Educational, 1966); and, Anthony E Bottoms, 'An Introduction to the "Coming Crisis"', in Anthony E Bottons and R H Preston (eds), *The Coming Penal Crisis* (Edinburgh, Scottish Academic Press, 1980).

3. Paul Rock, *Helping Victims of Crime: The Home Office and the Rise of Victim Support in England and Wales* (Oxford, Oxford University Press, 1990), 36.

4. op. cit. n.1, p. 143; Michael Moriarty was in charge of criminal policy between 1975-79, and he was largely responsible for *A Review of Criminal Justice Policy 1976* (London, HMSO., 1977; see also, C J Train, 'The Development of Criminal Policy Planning in the Home Office', *Public Administration* (1977): 373-384.

5. Andrew Rutherford, *Prisons and the Process of Justice* (Oxford, Oxford University Press, 1986), 56.

6. Home Office, *A Review of Criminal Justice Policy 1976* (London, HMSO, 1970), 7; Michael Moriarty was quite explicit about this, commenting that the Home Office had tended to neglect the judiciary in its various deliberations; he also somewhat wryly remarked that in the years that immediately followed the setting up of the Unit, the prison population rose, having fallen in the years immediately before, op. cit. n.l, pp. 141-142.

7. See, Richard Crossman, *The Diaries of a Cabinet Minister. Volume Three* (London, Hamish Hamilton and Jonathan Cape, 1977), 47.

8. D E R Faulkner, 'The redevelopment of Holloway Prison', *Howard Journal of Penology and Crime Prevention*, 13 (1971): 122-132; see also Paul Rock, 'The Opening Stages of Criminal Justice Policy Making', *British Journal of Criminology*, 35 (1995): 1-16.

9. See for example, Andrew Rutherford, 'Workshops: Linking the institution and urban area', *Prison Service Journal*, 14, (1973): 1-6.

10. The Criminal and General Departments later became the criminal policy and criminal justice and constitutional departments, and the statistical department and the research and planning unit became the research and statistics department.

11. op. cit. n. 3, p. 416.

12. Paul Rock, 'The Social Organization of a Home Office Initiative', *European Journal of Criminal Law and Criminal Justice* 2 (1994), 143.

13. Lord Windlesham, *Responses to Crime Volume Two Penal Policy in the Making* (Oxford, Oxford University Press, 1993), x.

14. Roy D King and Kathleen McDermott, *The State of our Prisons* (Oxford, Oxford University Press, 1995), 3-4; the author was also a member of the discussion groups throughout this period. On occasion the group would be attended by overseas visitors. For example Hans Tulkens, the director the Dutch prison service, has commented to the author that he attended two such meetings and could not envisage a similar group of professionals in the Netherlands finding the time to attend meetings of this sort; but compare Patrik Törnudd's description of a somewhat similar group in Finland in Chapter 5.

15. op. cit. n. 13, p. 8.

16. Interview with David Faulkner, January, 1990.

17. William Whitelaw, *The Whitelaw Memoirs* (London, Aurum Press, 1989), 221-227.

18. Interview with David Faulkner, January 1990.

19. William Whitelaw, speech to Leicestershire Magistrates' Association, 13 February, 1981.

20. In March 1982 Mr Whitelaw told the House of Commons: 'We are determined to ensure that there will be room in the prison system for every person whom the judges and magistrates decide should go there, and we will continue to do whatever is necessary for that purpose.' (*H C Debs. Sixth Series*, vol. 21, col. 1122, 25 March 1982). He repeated this phrase, with much emphasis, at the Conservative Party Conference seven months later.

21. Andrew Rutherford, *Growing out of Crime* (Winchester, Waterside Press, 1992), 16-17.

22. The Criminal Justice Act 1982 also provided for earlier discretionary release, and mandatory legal representation as a pre-requisite to custodial sentences for young offenders. At least government was listening to informed arguments for reform, and in 1983 the DHSS (as it then was) announced a fifteen million pound scheme to support 'intermediate treatment' programmes providing the courts with well organized alternatives to custody and care orders when dealing with juvenile offenders.

23. op. cit. n. 17, p. 307.

24. The official papers for this period will not be available for many years and civil service rules prevent many of the actual participants from making public their reflections on the period. Consequently, these speeches are an especially rich source of material on criminal policy-making as well as charting the development

of Faulkner's own thinking. The period of Faulkner's speeches begins in 1981 when he was in his last year at the Prison Department and ends shortly after he left the criminal policy department and moved to head the Establishments division. A dozen or so of the one hundred and twenty speeches were subsequently published in practictioner journals. All the speeches were kindly made available by Mr Faulkner to the author.

25. Faulkner retained responsibility for a while after he moved to the Establishments division in October 1990 for the Home Office 'special conferences', which he regarded as useful in terms of addressing contemporary criminal justice issues and also, at least in a small and tentative way, of encouraging 'continuous evaluation and adjustment of criminal policy'.

26. op. cit. n. 8, p. 5.

27. Faulkner further commented that the memorandum by Lord Armstrong, the head of the civil service, on the role of civil servants had always seemed to him to concentrate too much on the passive and negative aspects of the job.

28. For example, in May 1983 talking to chief probation officers he used the contrasting headings 'punitivists' and 'social interventionists'. He made the cryptic observation that if the former theme was to dominate, there would be little room for probation. On the other hand the latter theme held the promise of a significant role for the probation service at the centre.

29. Home Office, *Criminal Justice: A Working Paper* (London, Home Office, 1984).

30. A Keith Bottomley, 'Blue-Prints for Criminal Justice: Reflections on a Policy Plan for the Netherlands', *Howard Journal of Criminal Justice*, 25 (1986), 213.

31. It was the particularly shrill tone of Brittan's speech to the Party faithful which must have alarmed officials, fearful that it would destroy any tactical advantage being played for by the home secretary. Indeed, in the harsher penal climate of the next few years the rate of increase in the prison population rose sharply despite the accelerated early release of short-term prisoners (section 33 of the Criminal Justice Act 1982 which was activated in July 1984) and Court of Appeal guidelines aimed at keeping petty offenders out of prison(*Upton*(1980) 71 *Cr.App.R* 102; and *Bibi* (1980) 2 *Cr.App.R* (S) 177). David Faulkner later acknowledged that among the influences upon sentencing practice during the 1980s was 'Mr Leon Brittan's speech to the Conservative Party Conference in October 1983 which seems to have cancelled the effect of *Upton* and *Bibi*'.

32. Towards the end of the 1980s Faulkner and his Home Office colleagues were convinced that only by changing the language would sentencers be encouraged to view 'community penalties' as the appropriate sentence rather than as an alternative to prison.

33. This theme was being carefully explored by Andrew Ashworth; see Andrew Ashworth, 'Judicial Independence and Sentencing Reform' (paper presented at

the Cambridge Criminology Conference, July 1979); see also, Andrew Ashworth, *Sentencing and Penal Policy* (London, Weidenfeld and Nicolson, 1983), 58-97.

34. Two of Lord Justice Woolf's assessors were close associates of Faulkner. Mary Tuck had recently retired as head of the Home Office research and planning unit, and Rod Morgan of Bristol University was a member of the discussion groups which Faulkner organized between 1980-90, as was Mrs Tuck from the mid-1980s.

35. *Raymond v. Honey* (1982) *All ER* 756.

36. However, fourteen months later, in April 1984, Leon Brittan announced that work on the code had been abandoned. This work on prison standards was an early recognition that progress on normalizing prisons was more likely to be achieved through the courts than through the political process, as indeed was borne out in the experience of the United Kingdom in terms of its obligations under the European Convention on Human Rights. For a recent discussion, see for example, Bert Swart and James Young, 'The European Convention on Human Rights and Criminal Justice in The Netherlands and the UK.' in Christoper Harding, Phil Fennell, Nico Jörg and Bert Swart, (eds), *Criminal Justice in Europe: A Comparative Study* (Oxford, Oxford University Press, 1995), 57-86.

37. Doubts within the Home Office about incapacitation as an instrument of criminal policy had been in large part confirmed by a key study at the start of the decade. See, Stephen Brody and Roger Tarling, *Taking Offenders out of Circulation* Home Office Research Study, No. 64 (London, HMSO 1980). It is extraordinary that the views of James Q Wilson and other American supporters of incapacitation did not make more headway in Britain at that time. Margaret Thatcher has acknowledged Wilson's influence upon her own reflections about crime. Margaret Thatcher, *Margaret Thatcher, The Path To Power* (London, Harper Collins, 1995, 542n and 557n.) But in *The Downing Street Years*, she has nothing to say about Douglas Hurd's approach to criminal policy, and appeared to show little interest except with regard to the question of contracting out prison management to the private sector. But as Lord Windlesham notes, even this interest had more to do with her broader ideological agenda than any particular view about prisons. op. cit n. 13, pp. 421-422.

38. Conservative Party Manifesto, *The Next Moves Forward* (London, Conservative Party Central Office, 1987), 55. The team of seven senior ministers set up to supervise the manifesto also included William Whitelaw.

39. op. cit. n. 13, p. 210.

40. ibid., 215. Lord Windlesham correctly emphasises the role played by Douglas Hurd, especially during his 'Indian summer' of 1987 to 1989. For a pivotal statement of Hurd's 'one nation' approach to criminal policy see his speech celebrating the Centennial of Sir Robert Peel's birth to the Peel Society, Tamworth, 5 February 1988.

41. ibid., 211; John Patten was minister of state at the Home Office from June 1987 until April 1992 when he was promoted to Secretary of State for Education.

He returned to the backbenches in 1994. Among the officials present at the seminar was Michael Moriarty, who was then Establishments Officer in the Home Office.

42. Andrew von Hirsch, *Doing Justice: The Choice of Punishments* Report of the Committee for the Study of Incarceration (New York, Hill and Wang, 1976); see also, Andrew von Hirsch, *Past or Future Crimes: Deservedness and Dangerousness in the Sentencing of Criminals* (New Brunswick, New Jersey, Rutgers University Press, 1985).

43. Andrew Ashworth, 'Reducing the Prison Population in the 1980s: The Need for Sentencing Reform' (London, NACRO, 1982), 17; see also op. cit. n. 33 (1983), pp 222-224.

44. Home Office, *Punishment, Custody and The Community* Cm. 424 (London, HMSO, 1988), 8-9.

45. This specific target was repeated by Faulkner four days later in a talk on the green paper to the Grubb Institute; these references by Faulkner to a specific figure might be compared to the target he had earlier regarding the use of the probation service. Faulkner had very little to say about the other green paper, *Private Sector Involvement in the Remand System* (cm. 434, 1988) other than the issues it raised were for ministers to decide.

46. Faulkner took an early interest in reports that since the mid-1980s the prison population in the the Federal Republic of Germany had been declining. He met with leading German academics such as Johannes Feest of Bremem University, who spoke at NACRO's Annual General Meeting in 1988; see, Johannes Feest, *Reducing the Prison Population: Lessons from the West German Experience?* (London, NACRO, 1988); and with Christian Pfeiffer of Hannover University, who was brought to Britain on several occasions as a consultant by the Home Office). John Graham of the research and planning unit was asked to assess developments in Germany, especially with respect to young offenders; see, John Graham, 'Decarceration in the Federal Republic of Germany', *British Journal of Criminology*, 30 (1990): 150-170.

47. The term 'dependency culture' was much in vogue during the 1980s as the ethos of the welfare state was increasingly challenged by government; see, for example, David Hare in *The Observer* (15 October 1995).

48. Douglas Hurd (speech to the annual Conservative Party Conference, Blackpool, 11 October, 1989), 8-9.

49. op. cit. n. 13, pp. 242-245.

50. Home Office, *Crime, Justice and Protecting The Public. The Government's Proposals for Legislation* Cm. 965 (London, HMSO, 1990), 6.

51. op. cit. n. 13, p. 462.

52. Home Office, *The Parole System in England and Wales* report of the Review Committee Cm 532 (London, H.M.S.O., 1988).

53. The number of juveniles (persons aged 10-16) found guilty of indictable offences by courts in England and Wales between 1980-1990 declined from 90200 to 24700; custodial sentences for 14-16 year olds fell from 7500 to 1445 over the same period. See generally, Rutherford, op. cit. n. 21, pp. 11-27.

54. Basingstoke and Northampton were two of the communities where the new approaches to juvenile justice were first developed; ibid., 112-120.

55. This national initiative owed much of its impetus to the government's 'Three E's' of Efficiency, Economy and Effectiveness. The Financial Management Initiative was pre-tested in twelve probation service areas.

56. In these remarks, Faulkner drew upon Anthony E Bottoms and William W McWilliams, 'A non-treatment paradigm for probation practice', *British Journal of Social Work*, 9 (1979), 159-202.

57. David Garland, 'Critical Reflections on the Green Paper' in Huw Rees and Eryl Hall Williams (eds), *Punishment, Custody and the Community. Reflections and Comments on the Green Paper* (London, London School of Economics, 1989), 14.

58. Home Office Circular, 8/84.

59. Ronald V G Clarke and Patricia Mayhew, *Designing Out Crime* (London, HMSO, 1980). For a later treatment, see Ronald V G Clarke (ed), *Situational Crime Prevention* (New York, Harrow and Heston, 1992).

60. Tim Hope and Margaret Shaw, 'Community approaches to reducing crime' in Tim Hope and Margaret Shaw (eds), *Communities and Crime Reduction* (London, HMSO, 1988), 1-29; see also Mary Tuck, 'Community and the Criminal Justice System', *Policy Studies,* 12 (1991), 22-37. Mary Tuck played a key role in bringing these research findings to the attention of ministers.

61. Hugo Young, *One Of Us, A Biography of Margaret Thatcher* (London, Macmillan, 1989), 538.

62. The Home Office Standing Committee on Crime Prevention (the Morgan Report) also urged in 1991 that local authorities play the lead role on crime prevention, but this remained an alien concept to ministers as a whole.

63. Michael King of Brunel University was asked by members of the Home Office research and planning unit to assess crime prevention developments in France. In his fascinating report, King found that crime prevention projects in France had been 'remarkably successful in uniting the mainstream political parties of both right and left and in generating cooperation among government departments, both centrally and locally, and between the state and charitable organizations. It is as if "crime prevention" has become the pass-word which has enabled all manner of doors to be opened and all kinds of barriers to be lowered.'

Michael King, *How to Make Social Crime Prevention Work. The French Experience* (London, NACRO, 1988), 36.

64. op. cit. n. 13, p. 213.

65. op. cit. n. 3, p. 415.

66. ibid., 408.

67. When the white paper was published there was some concern that the Government was insufficiently sensitive to the discriminatory bias across the criminal justice process. At a conference in Stratford, which took place in October 1990, it was agreed that the legislation should address these issues as directly as possible. However, what emerged was a much watered down clause, eventually becoming section 95 of the Criminal Justice Act 1991. This provided that the Secretary of State publish, on an annual basis, information for the purpose of facilitating the performance of criminal justice practitioners in avoiding discrimination on grounds of race or sex or any other improper ground. With respect to the broader aspects of equal opportunities, Faulkner explained that his focus was mostly upon race rather than gender issues because the stakes were higher, the prejudices ran deeper and the problems of communication were more serious.

CHAPTER 5

The Limits of Criminal Policy

Criminal policy developments since the early 1980s have been characterised by the encroachment of both managerial and populist influences on humanitarian and legal values. To the extent that there has been a challenge to the managerial agenda in The Netherlands, it appears not to have extended much beyond academic lawyers. By the mid-1990s the direction ahead for Dutch criminal policy remain uncertain. There are few, if any, traces of uncertainty with respect to criminal policy in the United States, where the pace set in the mid-1970s has accelerated. The extent to which crime issues have become deeply politicised was borne out in the presidential election campaigns of 1992 and in the mid-term elections two years later. The 'three strikes and you're out', 'truth in sentencing', and associated provisions in the Violent Crime Control and Law Enforcement Act of 1994 have been matched or exceeded in several states. A close observer of the American scene has commented, with reference to the federal legislation, that prisons, 'arguably our most spectacular failed social experiment, get a free lunch; prevention gets the shaft, forced again to fight for every penny year after year, even though we know it can work.'[1]

The escalation in prison and jail populations in the United States which began in the early 1970s has shown no signs of slowing down, and in this respect appears to differ from previous periods of sudden growth. All natural tendencies towards stability appear to have evaporated. Not only has there been a quantum leap of unprecedented proportions in prison populations, but there appear also to be no indications of any counter forces which might impose limits. There is general agreement among scholars that once criminal policy in the United States had fallen into the political arena there was, as Alfred Blumstein has noted, 'little that could be done to recapture concern for limiting prison populations.'[2] He added that 'our political system learned an overly simplistic trick: when it responds to such pressures by sternly demanding increased punishments, that approach has been found to be strikingly effective - not in solving the problem, but in alleviating the political pressure to "do something".'[3]

While there are individual scholars and a few independent organizations calling for a more reflective and humane approach to criminal policy, these voices have been muffled in the political crusade for harsher measures against offenders. Yet that is not the way it is seen by the professor of politics at Princeton University, John J DiIulio, who has contended that

> (b)y every measure, the anti-incarceration élite has been winning its tug-of-war with the public on crime . . . America has crime without punishment . . . get-tough politics is good crime policy . . . (the President should) brook no nonsense from Democratic congressmen who demand more money for Great Society retreads as the price of their support for serious anti-crime measures.[4]

DiIulio's voice is shriller than that of his mentor, James Q Wilson, but he seems certain nevertheless to consolidate his reputation to be the academic most in tune with the movement towards an ever more authoritarian approach to criminal policy. Leon Radzinowicz, the distinguished British criminologist and a United States resident, has written that he had no hesitation in affirming 'that the American system belongs to the lowest category among the democratic countries of the world.'[5] In similar vein, Nils Christie of Oslo University, in his international survey of contemporary criminal policy, described the United States as the 'trend setter', with increasingly large numbers of those who are regarded as 'core members of the dangerous population . . . confined, warehoused, stored away, and forced to live their active years as consumers of control. It can be done democratically and under the strict control of legal institutions.'[6] In the first edition of Christie's 1993 book, *Crime Control as Industry*, the subtitle was 'Towards Gulags, Western Style?' When the revised version of the book was published two years later the question mark had been removed.

The unfolding of criminal policy in England and Wales in the 1990s has been especially eventful. When, in October 1990, David Faulkner warned of the dangers of a 'punitive reaction' he cannot have anticipated the ferocity of the *volte face* which was only two or three years away. With the passage of the Criminal Justice Act in the early summer of 1991, the way forward for criminal policy for a decade or more seemed largely set. For all its limitations, the Act represented an unusually comprehensive attempt to construct a coherent approach to sentencing. Its overriding rationale was to provide sentencers with a principled framework which would encourage proportionality between the seriousness of the offence and the severity of the sentence. Although any estimate of the legislation's impact upon the prison

126

population was highly problematic, there was certainly the intent that a wider use be made of community penalties in sentencing repeat property offenders. In short, as Andrew Ashworth observed, the 1991 Act went 'further than any other modern English sentencing legislation in trying to impose a structure on the sentencing decisions of the courts.'[7] The Criminal Justice Act 1991 was but one feature of a more coherent approach to criminal policy which emerged from developments during the 1980s. Lord Justice Woolf's far-reaching report on the prison disturbances of April 1990 was largely accepted in the white paper, *Custody, Care and Justice* which was presented to Parliament in September 1991. Thereby, an agenda for prison reform was set that extended well into the next century. To these policy signposts might be added a series of reports issued by a joint Home Office and Department of Health working party on mentally disordered offenders, as well as further encouragement to the police to caution rather than prosecute certain categories of offenders. For a brief period it looked as though this new calm and reflective approach might be held together. During 1992, for example, there was a further substantial decline in the prison population, much of it ahead of the Act's sentencing provisions, yet to be implemented.

But by the early Spring of 1993 it was clear that a number of countervailing forces were gaining ground rapidly. First, the police led a sophisticated campaign on the issue of persistent juvenile offenders, quickly converted by the media into a moral panic and prompting a new home secretary, Kenneth Clarke, to announce that 'secure training centres' would be provided to hold children as young as twelve years old. The second source of pressure came from the judiciary which lost no time in voicing opposition to those aspects of the legislation which restricted their discretion in taking account of previous convictions. In an unusual attack on a statute in force for only six months, the Lord Chief Justice complained that judges had been placed in an 'ill-fitting straightjacket'.[8] A third and perhaps most significant development was the sea-change that occured among senior politicians within both main political parties. While there had been earlier hints of these shifts, the new political discourse became evident immediately after the General Election of April 1992. Arriving at the Home Office, Kenneth Clarke did little to avoid the impression that he was unhappy not only with the Criminal Justice Act 1991 but with the generally liberal course that had been pursued in the latter part of the 1980s. He was also only too well aware that his opposite number on the Labour Party benches, Tony Blair, was in the process of stealing his party's 'law and order' mantle. The new Labour catchphrase, 'tough on crime, tough on the

127

causes of crime', became one more pressure on the government to repudiate its carefully constructed criminal policy. The Criminal Justice Act 1993, which amended core sections of the 1991 legislation and the Criminal Justice and Public Order Act 1994, put the statutory seal on the dramatic change of direction. In the course of his '27 points' speech to the Conservative Party Conference in October 1993, Mr Clarke's successor, Michael Howard declared: 'Let us be clear. Prison works. It ensures that we are protected from murderers, muggers and rapists - and it will make many who are tempted to commit crimes think twice.'[9] The shrill tone adopted by ministers was reflected in day-to-day practice. Prison numbers, having declined between 1988-1992, began to rise sharply and within two years had exceeded previous record highs.

Among the critics of the Home Office policy 'U-turn' was David Faulkner, having taken up an academic post at Oxford University. Faulkner described the change in the government's policies on crime and criminal justice as 'the most sudden and the most radical which has ever taken place in this area of public policy.' He continued:

> The fact is that there is now a serious void at the centre of the criminal justice system. There is no clearly understood set of purposes which it is meant to achieve or principles which it is meant to observe, and no effective and acceptable system of accountability for its operation . . . Without a greater sense of purpose and direction, the prospect is one of increasing frustration and anger, a spiral of rising crime, increasing severity of punishment and the alienation of a growing section of the community.[10]

At a Ditchley Foundations conference on 'Penal Policy: Punishments, Prisons and Crime Prevention' which took place in February 1994, Faulkner observed that the predominant view of governments in Britain and the United States was associated with a perspective on crime and criminality which distinguished between a deserving, blameless, law-abiding citizenry on the one hand and a dangerous, hostile, criminal class on the other.

> Those who held this view believed that it was the task of the criminal justice services, and the criminal justice process as a whole, to protect law-abiding citizens from the criminal classes, in a conflict which was often described in the language of warfare. This instrumentalist view of the criminal justice system did not however take adequate account of the fact that many crimes were a spontaneous reaction to a situation or opportunity, in which rational choice played a very small part. It was also

damaging to the values enshrined in the notion of criminal justice itself -
the presumption of innocence, due process and equality before the law.[11]

Faulkner's attendance at the Ditchley conference must have reminded
him of the occasion less than five years previously when, in the same
surroundings, Home Office ministers and civil servants met with
senior judges to discuss the outlines of the planned legislation. He
might well have asked himself whether the approach to criminal
policy which had been pursued was hopelessly misguided, and
whether there were more that might have been done to protect it
against forces pulling in the opposite direction.

In recent years Nils Christie and Thomas Mathiesen, both based at
Oslo University, have in their separate writings made an enormous
contribution to our understanding of the fragility of, to use Leon
Radzinowicz's term, the 'socio-liberal model of criminal policy'.[12] The
complementary insights generated in the work of these two
distinguished Norwegian criminologists provide an invaluable
framework for assessing the competing strands which drive any
transformation of criminal policy.

The starting place is Christie's concept of the 'joint moral
community' which, under specified conditions, may be regarded as
consisting of those people who are responsible for shaping a society's
criminal policy. He suggests that there are four conditions which are
basic to the joint moral community. First, the joint moral community
encourages a scepticism about prisons as well as other aspects of
criminal policy; secondly, there is an insistence upon empathy with
offenders, 'the imaginative power, the capacity to see oneself in the
other person's situation'.[13] With this personal identification it becomes
more difficult to impose extreme measures. The third factor is the
adoption of an inclusive and not exclusive view of offenders. Most
offenders are 'people, ordinary people, not a special breed of
bandits,'[14] and finally, the joint moral community leads to agreement
about 'some kind of informal minimum standards for what is
considered decent to do in the name of punishment. These are
standards that are valid for *all* human beings.'[15] In the first instance,
the joint moral community depends upon the sustained commitment
and close involvement of an inner group of decision-makers,
consisting of experts and other élites. A good example of a joint moral
community has existed for some years in Finland, where the prison
population has fallen steadily since the late 1970s. Patrik Törnudd,
who has provided the fullest account, has written that

the fact that it became possible to carry out a large number of reforms aimed at reducing the level of punishment was ultimately dependent on the fact that the small group of experts who were in charge of reform planning or who worked as crime control experts in research institutes and universities shared an almost unanimous conviction that Finland's internationally high prisoner rate was a disgrace and that it would be possible to significantly reduce the amount and length of prison sentences without serious repercussions in the crime situation.[16]

Törnudd had no hesitation in concluding that the decisive factor in accounting for Finland's declining prison population has been

the attitudinal readiness of the civil servants, the judiciary and the prison authorities to use all available means in order to bring down the number of prisoners. *Through the efforts of a group of key individuals it had become possible to define Finland's prisoner rate as a problem* and that problem conception in turn produced a number of activities, ranging from law reforms to low level day-to-day decisions, which all contributed to the end result.[17]

This élite group, which shared an 'attitudinal and ideological readiness to bring down the number of prisoners', consisted of some twenty to twenty-five people, including supporters and fringe members. According to Törnudd, the core membership was, perhaps, little more than a half dozen people. They included Inkeri Anttila of the University of Helsinki and Karl-Johan Lång, director of the prison system. Many of those most directly involved used to attend an informal discussion group on criminal policy issues which met at Professor Anttila's home in the 1960s.[18]

Christie's notion of 'the joint moral community' also reaches out through a variety of networks so as to involve other key groups. The example he uses is a remarkable initiative instigated by Thomas Mathiesen. For more than twenty years, under the auspices of KROM, the Norwegian Association for Penal Reform, Mathiesen has organized an annual meeting over two or three days at a mountain retreat on the outskirts of Oslo. These meetings bring together criminal justice practitioners, politicians, the 'liberal opposition' (lay people with an interest in criminal policy), journalists and prisoners. Nils Christie, who has provided the fullest account of these meetings, attaches particular importance to the involvment in the meetings of serving prisoners.

Norway is a small country. Those with responsibility for running the formal system of crime control cannot avoid knowing each other, or at least of each other. They cannot escape their critics, and the critics cannot escape those with responsibility. We are forced into some degree of proximity . . . The participants are a select sample. Some upholders of stern law and strict order would not dream of participating up there in the mountains. But a sufficient number from all sections are there to create communication . . . (and) . . . to leak into the system a fundamental doubt as to the productivity of more prisons, as well as some doubts about the usefulness of the trend in Europe and in the United States in particular.[19]

Mathiesen has also described the work of KROM's meetings in the mountains and an attempt

to create *a network of opinion and information* crossing the formal and informal borders between segments of the relevant administration and political system. The point is precisely that of trying to create an alternative public sphere where argumentation and principled thinking are dominant values.[20]

The concept of an 'alternative public sphere' (which Mathiesen acknowledges is a rather cumbersome phrase when compared with the Norwegian *alternativ offentlighet*) serves as a crucial counter-weight to other public spheres, and in particular to the dominating role of the mass media. In earlier work, Mathiesen proposes that there are three important public spheres of influence in society, which are 'simultaneously, systems which supposedly perform the task of continually keeping institutions such as the prison under review and control.'[21] Although he developed his model with a particular focus on the 'pervasive and persistent ideology of prison', it is also applicable to aspects of the wider criminal policy arena. Mathiesen's three spheres, the 'outer', the 'inner' and the 'kernal' feedback circles may be briefly summarised as follows: the widest of the three public spheres is the 'outer public sphere' and includes the whole range of modern mass media. Within this sphere, with regard to imprisonment, Mathiesen suggests that there is a continual *non-recognition* of the 'fiasco' of the prison. The received wisdom is that imprisonment provides a solution to crime. According to Mathiesen, '(t)he notion of the general preventive effect of punishment is so deeply ingrained in the "common sense thinking" of society, that questions about its actual existence are frequently not raised and remain unasked.'[22] James Q Wilson, for example, is clearly at home within this sphere with his successful efforts to redefine the scope and direction of American public policy on crime. As a political scientist with a hobby horse on crime, his successful mission was to challenge 'what the few now think rather than what the many long believed'.

The narrower 'inner' public sphere consists of the institutions directly engaged in dealing with crime, such as the police, prosecutors, courts and the prison service. In this sphere, Mathiesen suggests that the problem is one of *pretence,* so that with regard to the prison 'the participants pretend that the prison is a success, though in fact it is not and they more or less know it.' In the absence of this pretence 'much of the work done by people and institutions within this sphere would appear meaningless and counterproductive.'[23] It is within this sphere that senior practitioners are likely to be most influential as exemplified by the redefinition of criminal policy in The Netherlands by Dato Steenhuis and others within a managerialist ideology. The narrowest or 'kernal' public sphere includes professional groups such as senior civil servants and researchers. Again, following Mathiesen's model, while there is *non-recognition* and *pretence* with regard to the 'fiasco' of the prison it is difficult for these to be maintained and it is *disregard* which takes over. David Faulkner was located within this sphere and having overcome institutional inclinations towards *disregard* together with key colleagues he was able to tackle 'pretence' and non-recognition in the other spheres.

As Mathiesen emphasises, these spheres are not self-contained; the boundaries are perforated in many places and there is considerable interaction among them. As a result, the pretence in the 'inner sphere' feeds into the non-recognition pattern in the 'outer sphere', and the disregard in the 'kernal' may spill into the other spheres. As was noted earlier, Mathiesen was interested in accounting for the obstinate survival of the prison, but his model can also be used as a means of tracing the influences which shape criminal policy, including those exerted by the joint moral community. His recent emphasis on the need for an 'alternative public sphere' is one attempt to do just this. The 'alternative public' sphere may thereby be regarded as a vehicle by which the joint moral community is able to reach across the three public spheres of influence.

The notion of a joint moral community provides a useful framework for considering aspects of criminal policy-making described in the preceding chapters. It may be argued that David Faulkner was involved in generating, sustaining and defending a joint moral community. He was, of course, constrained by his civil service status, having therefore to operate within relatively narrow public spheres. He was able to take forward several themes, however, which were not necessarily new, but which needed to be linked together within a semblance of coherent policy. From his academic base, James Q Wilson was better positioned to exert influence across the various spheres. Wilson was a populist with a difference. He saw his mission as changing élite opinion about crime so that it became closer to the views of ordinary people. Faulkner, on the other hand, sought to strengthen the leadership role of élites in setting the criminal policy agenda. Steenhuis, operating within the narrowest sphere, was able to supplant the traditionally humanistic joint moral community which had held together for a generation or more. As Nils Christie has warned, 'a system based on tolerance from above is a vulnerable one.'[24]

The events described in the previous chapters underline the increasingly fragile state of the joint moral community. This is, in part, a consequence of populist pressures which carry the seductive promise that the solution lies with more authoritarian measures. Nils Christie is astutely aware of the dangers inherent in the democratisation of criminal policy with its encouragement of organizations once fairly mute to become active and often sophisticated lobbyists. Similarly, Thomas Mathiesen has drawn attention to the degree that criminal policy has become a 'commodity' in recent times. Some years ago, criminal policy-making was at least to some limited extent governed by general, theoretical, philosophical and even scientific concerns.[25] Contemporary criminal policy-making

is governed much more by the particular definitions, interests and wishes - one might even say whims - of the police (or those representing police values), by those kinds of news which are newsworthy and thereby saleable for the media and by what is marketable in view of the currents of the political climate.[26]

This marketable criminal policy 'is founded on highly indirect, selective and skewed information filtered through the mass media, its alleged democratic aspects become suspect to say the least. The commodity character of today's (criminal) policy explains the erratic repressiveness which is so characteristic of contemporary decision-making in the area.'[27]. Legitimation has in turn become opportunistic: what 'goes' in the media and with the voters. But, as Mathiesen goes on correctly to observe, there has also been a change in the nature of the public debate over criminal policy. Communicative rationality, which was to some extent once present, now more than ever

lives its life in the secluded corners of the professional journals and meetings, while the public debate, flooded as it is with dire warnings from

133

the police, sensational crime stories, and opportunistic political initiatives, is predominantly characterized by the rationality of the market place.[28]

Alongside the popularisation of criminal policy are influences arising from a managerialist ideology which is, of course, all too evident in many areas of public policy. 'The virtue of managerialism', Carol Jones has acutely observed, is that 'it is divorced from any substantive normative or political values. Indeed, it transforms the absence of principled policy (for example, along the lines of justice and fairness) from a vice into a virtue.'[29] In the criminal policy arena, the new cult of managerialism serves to reinforce pragmatic expediency.[30]

In the 1990s the role of the joint moral community in shaping criminal policy has become ever more precarious. The combination of populist agenda and the pressures of managerialism have combined to dilute, if not dismantle, those limits which protect society from the pursuit of ever more simplistic and authoritarian solutions. These contemporary tendencies pose complex challenges to people within liberal democracies who are determined to do something about crime without making matters worse.

ENDNOTES

1. Elliott Currie, 'What's Wrong With the Crime Bill', *The Nation* (31 January, 1994), 121; see also, Marc Mauer, 'The Fragility of Criminal Justice Reform', *Social Justice,* 21 (1994): 14-29. With reference to the Crime Bill, Mauer writes that 'by promoting a mix of punishment and prevention, the (Clinton) administration was attempting to bring together the left and right on these issues. The problem with this strategy is that by 1994, there was not an equal need for both punishment and prevention. Twenty years of 'get tough' policies along with declining support for social welfare programs had created a decaying urban economy and community, and a bloated prison system. By failing to confront these trends and to challenge the assumptions upon which they were based the advocacy of punishment mixed with prevention remains vulnerable to being attacked as "soft on crime".' (ibid., 23).

2. Alfred Blumstein, 'Prisons' in James Q Wilson and Joan Petersilia (eds), *Crime* (San Francisco, Institute for Contemporary Studies, 1995), 397.

3. ibid., 399.

4. John J DiIulio, 'Let 'em Rot', *The Wall Street Journal* (January 26, 1994).

5. Leon Radzinowicz, 'Penal Regressions', *The Cambridge Law Journal* 50 (1993), 439.

6. Nils Christie, *Crime Control as Industry Towards Gulags Western Style?* (London and New York, Routledge, 1993), 171.

7. Andrew Ashworth, *Sentencing and Criminal Justice* (London, Weidenfeld and Nicolson, 1993), 43.

8. Lord Taylor, speech to the Law Society of Scotland, Gleneagles (March, 1993).

9. Michael Howard, speech to the annual conference of the Conservative Party, Blackpool (October, 1993).

10. David Faulkner, 'All Flaws and Disorder', *The Guardian* (11 November, 1993).

11. David Faulkner, 'Essay on a Ditchley Foundations Conference' in *Penal Policy: Punishments, Prisons and Crime Prevention* (February, 1994), 2.

12. op. cit. n. 5, p. 427.

13. op. cit. n. 6, p. 40.

14. ibid., 36.

15. ibid., 40.

16. Patrik Törnudd, *Fifteen Years of Decreasing Prisoner Rates in Finland* (Helsinki, National Research Institute of Legal Policy, 1993), 5.

17. ibid., 19 (emphasis added).

18. Personal communication to the author from Patrik Törnudd, 14 May, 1994.

19. op. cit. n. 6, pp. 39-40.

20. Thomas Mathiesen, 'Driving Forces Behind Prison Growth: The Mass Media' (paper presented to the International Conference on Prison Growth, Oslo, 28 April, 1995), 13 (emphasis in the orginal).

21. Thomas Mathiesen, *Prison on Trial A Critical Assessment* (London, Sage, 1990), 139.

22. ibid., 48-49.

23. ibid., 140.

24. op. cit. n. 6, p. 43.

25. Mathiesen uses the term 'penal policy' in these passages, but his comments are also applicable to criminal policy as a whole.

26. Thomas Mathiesen, 'Contemporary Penal Policy: A Study in Moral Panics' (speech to the Annual Meeting of the Howard League for Penal Reform, London, 25 November, 1992), 10.

27. ibid.; a further aspect has been highlighted by Zimring and Hawkins who comment that it may have become more difficult to make prison policy choices 'off-stage' in the 1990s. 'With recent developments in information systems and a new atmosphere of accountability, we may have passed the time when correctional policies could remain a political secret in state government. Indeed, this new feature of the political landscape may be one reason why correctional populations have soared.' Franklin E Zimring and Gordon Hawkins, 'The Growth of Imprisonment in California', *British Journal of Criminology*, 34 (1994), 280.

28. op. cit. n. 26, p. 11.

29. Carol Jones, *British Journal of Criminology*, 'Auditing Criminal Justice', 33 (1993), 201. Nicola Lacey has commented that 'all too often the actual specification of the relevant goals and values is avoided, being obscured with a discourse in which efficiency appears to become the end as well as the means.' Nicola Lacey, 'Government as Manager, Citizen as Consumer: The Case of the Criminal Justice Act 1991', *Modern Law Review,* 57 (1994), 534.

30. Andrew Rutherford, *Criminal Justice and the Pursuit of Decency* (Winchester, Waterside Press, 1994).

Bibliography

Abt Associates, *American Prisons and Jails, Volume 1, Summary Findings and Policy Implications*, (Washington DC, US Government Printing Office, 1980).

Alper, Benedict, 'Thinking About Crime', *Crime and Delinquency*, 22 (1976): 486-488.

Ancel, Marc, 'The relationship between criminology and "Politique Criminelle"' in Roger Hood (ed), *Crime, Criminology and Public Policy Essays in Honour of Sir Leon Radzinowicz* (London, Heinemann, 1974), 269-280.

Ashworth, Andrew, 'Principles, Practice and Criminal Justice' in Peter Birks (ed), *Pressing Problems of the Law, Volume 1, Criminal Justice and Human Rights* (Oxford, Oxford University Press, 1995), 43-45.
____, *The Criminal Process. An Evaluative Study* (Oxford, Oxford University Press, 1994)
____, *Sentencing and Criminal Justice* (London, Weidenfeld and Nicolson, 1992).
____, *Sentencing and Penal Policy* (London, Weidenfeld and Nicolson, 1983).
____, 'Reducing the Prison Population in the 1980s: The Need for Sentencing Reform' (London, NACRO, 1982).

Attorney General's Task Force on Violent Crime, *Final Report* (Washington, DC, US Department of Justice, 1981).

Banfield, Edward C, and James Q Wilson, *City Politics* (Cambridge, Massachusetts, Harvard University Press and the M I T Press, 1963).

Bayer, Ronald, 'Crime, Punishment, and the Decline of Liberal Optimism', *Crime and Delinquency*, 27 (1981): 169-190.

Beijerse, Jolande uit, and René van Swaaningen, 'Social Control as a Policy: Pragmatic Moralism with a Structural Deficit', *Social and Legal Studies*, 2 (1993): 281-302.

Blad, John R 'Selected Issues on Crime and Punishment in The Netherlands' (unpublished paper, Erasmus University, Rotterdam, 1992).

Blumstein, Alfred, 'Prisons' in James Q Wilson and Joan Petersilia (eds), *Crime* (San Francisco, Institute for Contemporary Studies, 1995), 387-419.
____, Jacqueline Cohen, Jeffrey A Roth, and Christy A Visher (eds), *Criminal Careers and 'Career Criminals'*, Volumes 1 and 2, (Washington, D C, National Research Council, National Academy Press, 1986).
____, Jacqueline Cohen and Daniel Nagin, *Deterrence and Incapacitation*, Report of the National Academy of Sciences Panel on Deterrent and Incapacitative Effects (Washington, D C, National Research Council, National Academy Press, 1978).
____, and R Larson, 'Models of a Total Criminal Justice System', *Operations Research*, 17 (1969): 199-231.

Boland, Barbara and James Q Wilson, 'Age, crime and punishment', *The Public Interest*, 51 (1978): 22-34.

Bottomley, A Keith, 'Blue-Prints for Criminal Justice: Reflections on a Policy Plan for the Netherlands', *Howard Journal of Criminal Justice*, 25 (1986): 199-215.

Bottoms, Anthony E, 'An Introduction to the "Coming Crisis"' in Anthony E Bottoms and R H Preston (eds), *The Coming Penal Crisis* (Edinburgh, Scottish Academic Press, 1980).
____, and Simon Stevenson, 'What Went Wrong?: Criminal Justice Policy in England and Wales, 1945-70' in David Downes (ed) *Unravelling Criminal Justice. Eleven British Studies* (London, Macmillan, 1992), 1-45.
____, and Paul Wiles, 'Crime and housing policy: a framework for crime prevention analysis' in Tim Hope and Mararet Shaw (eds) *Communities and Crime Reduction* (London, HMSO, 1988), 84-98.
____, and William W McWilliams 'A non-treatment paradigm for probation practice', *British Journal of Social Work*, 9 (1979): 159-202

Brody, Stephen and Roger Tarling, *Taking Offenders out of Circulation* Home Office Research Study, No 64 (London, HMSO, 1980).

Chaiken, Marcia R, and Jan M Chaiken, 'Offender Types and Public Policy', *Crime and Delinquency*, 30 (1984): 195-226.

Christie, Nils, *Crime Control as Industry. Towards Gulags Western Style ?* (London and New York, Routledge, 1993).

Clark, Ramsey, *Crime in America. Observations on its Nature, Causes, Prevention and Control* (New York, Simon and Schuster, 1970).

Clarke, Ronald V G and Patricia Mayhew, *Designing Out Crime* (London, HMSO, 1980).

Cloward, Richard A, and Lloyd E Ohlin, *Delinquency and Opportunity: A Theory of Delinquent Gangs* (New York, Free Press, 1960).

Crossman, Richard, *The Diaries of a Cabinet Minister. Volume Three* (London, Hamish Hamilton and Jonathan Cape, 1977).

Currie, Elliot, 'What's Wrong with the Crime Bill?', *The Nation* (31 January, 1994): 118-121.
____, 'Two Visions of Community Crime Prevention', in Tim Hope and Margaret Shaw (eds), *Communities and Crime Reduction* (London, HMSO, 1988), 280-286.
____, 'Reply to James Q Wilson', *Dissent* 33, (1985):227-229.

Curtis, Lynn A, *American Violence and Public Policy, An Update of the National Commission on the Causes and Prevention of Violence* (New Haven and London, Yale University Press, 1985).
____, 'The March of Folly - Crime and the Underclass' in Tim Hope and Margaret Shaw(eds), *Communities and Crime Reduction* London, HMSO,1988), 180-202.

DiIulio, John J, 'Crime in America: Three Ways to Prevent It'. Typescript of Congressional Testimony, (20 January 1995).

_____, 'The Question of Black Crime', *The Public Interest*, 117, (1994): 3-32.

_____, 'Crime' in Henry J Aaron and Charles L Schultze (eds), *Setting Domestic Priorities: What can Government Do?* (Washington, D C, Brookings, 1992), Chapter 4.

_____, 'James Q Wilson and Civic Virtue', *Political Science*, 24 (1991): 748-755.

_____, *Governing Prisons A Comparative Study of Correctional Management* (New York, Free Press, 1987).

_____, and Steven K Smith, and Aaron J Saiger, 'The Federal Role in Crime Control' in James Q Wilson and Joan Petersilia (eds), *Crime* (San Francisco, California, Institute for Contemporary Studies, 1995), 445-462.

Dijk, Jan J M van, 'Crime Prevention Policy: Current State and Prospects' in Gunther Kaiser and Hans-Jörg Albrecht (eds) *Crime and Criminal Policy in Europe. Proceedings of the 11. European Colloquium* (Freiburg, Max-Planck Institute, 1990), 205-220.

_____, Patricia Mayhew and M Killias, *Experience of Crime Across the World Key Findings of the 1989 International Crime Survey* (Deventer, Kluwer Law and Taxation Publishers, 1990).

Downes, David, *Contrasts in Tolerance, Post-War Penal Policy in the Netherlands and England and Wales* (Oxford, Oxford University Press, 1988).

European Committee on Crime Problems, *Conference on Criminal Policy* (Strasbourg, Council of Europe, 1975).

Faulkner, David, 'Essay on a Ditchley Foundations Conference', in *Penal Policy: Punishments, Prisons and Crime Prevention* (February, 1994), 1-7.

_____, 'All Flaws and Disorder', *The Guardian* (11 November, 1993).

_____, 'The redevelopment of Holloway Prison', *Howard Journal of Penology and Crime Prevention*, 13, (1971): 122-132.

Malcolm M Feeley, *Court Reform on Trial* (New York, Basic Books, 1983).

_____, and Jonathan Simon, 'Actuarial Justice: The Emerging New Criminal Law' in David Nelkin (ed) *The Futures of Criminology*, (London, Sage 1994), 173-201.

Feest, Johannes, *Reducing the Prison Population: Lessons from the West German Experience ?* (London, NACRO, 1988).

Fionda, Julia, *Public Prosecutors and Discretion: A Comparative Study* (Oxford, Oxford University Press, 1995).

Ford, Gerald R, *A Time To Heal, The Autobiography* (New York, Harper Row, 1979).

Garland, David, 'Critical Reflections on the Green Paper' in Huw Rees and Eryl Hall Williams (eds), *Punishment, Custody and the Community. Reflections and Comments on the Green Paper* (London, London School of Economics, 1989), 4-18.

Gordon, Diana R, *Doing Violence to the Violence Problems A Response to the Attorney General's Task Force* (Hackensack, New Jersey, National Council on Crime and Delinquency, 1981).

Gordon, Alan R, and Norval Morris, 'Presidential Commissions and the Law Enforcement Assistance Administration' in Lynn A Curtis (ed), *American Violence and Public Policy, An Update of the National Commission on the Causes and Prevention of Violence* (New Haven and London, Yale University Press, 1985), 117-132.

Gottfredson, Michael and Travis Hirschi, 'The True Value of Lambda would Appear to be Zero: An Essay on Career Criminals, Criminal Careers, Selective Incapacitation, Cohort Studies, and Related Topics', *Criminology*, 24 (1986): 213-234.

Graham, John, *Crime Prevention Strategies in Europe and North America* (Helsinki, Helsinki Institue for Crime Prevention and Control, 1990).
____, 'Decarceration in the Federal Republic of Germany', *British Journal of Criminology*, 30 (1990): 150-170.

Greenberg, David F and Drew Humphries, 'The Cooption of Fixed Sentencing Reform', *Crime and Delinquency*, 26 (1980): 210-225.

Greenwood, Peter W, and Allan Abrahamse, *Selective Incapacitation, Report prepared for the National Institute of Justice* (Santa Monica, California, Rand Corporation, 1982).
____, and Susan Turner, *Selective Incapacitation Revisited, Report prepared for the National Institute of Justice* (Santa Monica, California, Rand Corporation, 1987).

Haag van den, Ernst, *Punishing Criminals, Concerning a Very Old and Painful Question* (New York, Basic Books, 1975)

Haan, Willem de, *The Politics of Redress. Crime, Punishment and Penal Abolition* (London, Unwin Hyman, 1990).
____, 'Abolitionism and the Politics of "Bad Concience"', *Howard Journal of Criminal Justice*, 26 (1987): 15-32.
____, 'Explaining Expansion: the Dutch Case' (paper presented at the 13th Conference of the European Group for the Study of Deviance and Social Control, Hamburg, September 1985).

Haapeanen, Rudy, *Selective Incapacitation and the Serious Offender, A Longitudinal Study of Criminal Career Patterns* (New York, Springer-Verlag, 1990).

Hart, Auguste C 't, *Openbaar Ministerie en rechtshandhaving, Een verkenning* [Public Prosecution and Law Enforcement, An Exploration] (Arnhem, Gouda Quint, 1994).
____, 'Criminal Law Policy in The Netherlands' in Jan van Dijk, Charles Haffmans, Frits Rüter, Julian Schutte and Simon Stolwijk (eds). *Criminal Law in Action. An overview of current issues in Western societies* (Deventer, Kluwer Law and Taxation Publishers, 1988), 73-99.

140

Hecklo, Hugh, 'Reaganism and the Search for a Public Philosophy' in John L Palmer (ed), *Perspectives on the Reagan Years* (Washington, D C, The Urban Institute Press, 1986), 31-63.

Hirsch, Andrew von, *Past or Future Crimes: Deservedness and Dangerousness in the Sentencing of Criminals* (New Brunswick, New Jersey, Rutgers University Press, 1985).
____, *Doing Justice: The Choice of Punishments* Report of the Committee for the Study of Incarceration (New York, Hill and Wang, 1976).

Home Office, *Custody, Care and Justice: The Way Ahead for the Prison Service in England and Wales* Cm 1647 (London, HMSO, 1991).
____,*Crime, Justice and Protecting The Public. The Government's Proposals for Legislation* Cm 965 (London, HMSO, 1990).
____, *Punishment, Custody and The Community* Cm 424 (London, HMSO, 1988).
____, *Criminal Justice: A Working Paper* (London, Home Office, 1984).
____, *A Review of Criminal Justice Policy 1976* (London, HMSO, 1977).

Hood, Roger, 'Criminology and Penal Change: A Case Study of the Nature and Impact of some recent Advice to Governments' in Roger Hood (ed), *Crime, Criminology and Public Policy, Essays in Honour of Sir Leon Radzinowicz* (London, Heinemann, 1974), 375-417.

Hope, Tim and Margaret Shaw, 'Community approaches to reducing crime' in Tim Hope and Margaret Shaw (eds), *Communities and Crime Reduction* (London, HMSO, 1988), 1-29.

Jones, Carol, 'Auditing Criminal Justice', *British Journal of Criminology* 33 (1993): 187-202.

Jung, Heike, 'Criminal Justice - A European Perspective', *Criminal Law Review* (April 1993): 237-245.

Kelk, Constantijn, 'Criminal Justice in the Netherlands' in Phil Fennell, Christopher Harding, Nico Jörg, and Bert Swart (eds), *Criminal Justice in Europe. A Comparative Study* (Oxford, Oxford University Press, 1995), 1-20.

King, Michael, *How to Make Social Crime Prevention Work. The French Experience* (London, NACRO, 1988).

King, Roy D and Kathleen McDermott, *The State of our Prisons* (Oxford, Oxford University Press, 1995).

Lacey, Nicola, 'Government as Manager, Citizen as Consumer: The Case of the Criminal Justice Act 1991', *Modern Law Review* (57) : 534-554.

McMahon, Maeve, 'Crime, Justice and Human Rights in the Baltics' (paper presented at the International Conference on Prison Growth, Oslo, April, 1995).

Marris, Peter and Martin Rein, *Dilemmas of Social Reform, Poverty and Community Action in the United States* (New York, Atherton Press, 1967).

Mathiesen, Thomas, 'Driving Forces Behind Prison Growth: The Mass Media' (paper presented to the International Conference on Prison Growth, Oslo April, 1995).
____, *Prison on Trial A Critical Assessment* (London, Sage, 1990).
____, 'Contemporary Penal Policy: A Study in Moral Panics' (speech to the Annual General Meeting of the Howard League for Penal Reform, London, November, 1992).
____, 'The Future of Control Systems - the Case of Norway' in David Garland and Peter Young (eds), *The Power to Punish* (London, Heinemann Educational Books, 1983), 130-145.

Mauer, Marc, 'The Fragility of Criminal Justice Reform', *Social Justice* 21 (1994): 14-29.
____, and Tracy Huling, *Young Black Americans and the Criminal Justice System: Five Years Later* (Washington, D C, The Sentencing Project, 1995).

Mayer, William G, *The Changing American Mind, How and Why American Public Opinion Changed between 1960 and 1988* (Ann Arbor, The University of Michigan Press, 1992).

Miller, Jerome, *Last One Over The Wall: The Massachusetts Experiment in Closing Reform Schools* (Columbus, Ohio State University Press, 1991).

Miller, Alden D, and Lloyd E Ohlin, *Delinquency and Community, Creating Opportunities and Controls*, (Beverly Hills, Sage, 1985).

Ministerie van Justitie, *Werkzame detentie* [Effective Detention, Summary and Implementation], (The Hague, Ministry of Justice, 1994).
____, *Law in Motion. A policy plan for Justice in the years ahead* (The Hague, Ministry of Justice, 1990).
____, *Samenleving en Criminaliteit* [shortened English version *Society and Crime.A policy plan for The Netherlands*] (The Hague, Ministry of Justice, 1985).

Mintzberg, Henry, *The Structuring of Organizations* (Englewood Cliffs, Prentice Hall, 1979).

Moczydlowski, Pawel, 'Prison: From Communist System to Democracy. Transformation of the Polish Penitentiary System' (paper presented at the International Conference on Prison Growth, Oslo, April 1995).

Moore, Mark H, Susan R Estrich, Daniel McGillis and William Spelman (eds), *Dangerous Offenders, The Elusive Target of Justice* (Cambridge, Massachusetts and London, Harvard University Press, 1984).
Moriarty, Michael, 'The policy-making process: how it is seen from the Home Office' in Nigel Walker (ed), *Penal Policy-Making in England* (Cambridge, Institute of Criminology, 1977), 129-145.

Moynihan, Daniel P, *Maximum Feasible Misunderstanding, Community Action in the War on Poverty* (New York, The Free Press, 1970).

National Council for Crime Prevention, *Crime and Criminal Policy in Sweden 1985*, Report No 19, (Stockholm, National Council for Crime Prevention, 1985).

Openbaar Ministerie, *Strafrecht met belied: Beleidsplan Openbaar Ministerie 1990-1995* (The Hague, Openbaar Ministerie, 1990).

Peters, Antonie A G, 'Main Currents in Criminal Law Theory' in Jan van Dijk, Charles Haffmans, Frits Rüter, Julian Schutte and Simon Stolwwijk (eds), *Criminal Law in Action. An overview of current issues in Western Societies* (Deventer, Kluwer Law and Taxation Publishers, 1988), 19-36.

President's Commission on Law Enforcement and the Administration of Justice, *The Challenge of Crime in a Free Society* (Washington DC, US Government Printing Office, 1967).

Radzinowicz, Leon, 'Penal Regressions', *Cambridge Law Journal*, 50 (1991): 422-444.
____, *The Roots of the International Association of Criminal Law and their significance A Tribute and a re-assessment on the Centenary of the IKV* (Freiburg, Max-Planck Institute, 1991).
____, *Ideology and Crime. A study of Crime and its Social and Historical Context* (London, Heinemann Educational, 1966).

R. Rijksen, *Meningen van Gedetineerden over de Strafrechts-pleging* [Prisoners speak out] (Assen, van Gorcum, 1958).

Rock, Paul, 'The Opening Stages of Criminal Justice Policy Making', *British Journal of Criminology*, 35 (1995): 1-16.
____, 'The Social Organization of a Home Office Initiative', *European Journal of Criminal Law and Criminal Justice,* 2 (1994): 141-167.
____, *Helping Victims of Crime: The Home Office and the Rise of Victim Support in England and Wales* (Oxford, Oxford University Press, 1990).
____, Review of 'Thinking About Crime', *British Journal of Criminology*, 19 (1979): 80-81.

Rothman, David J, 'The Horrors of Prison Reform', *The New York Review of Books* (February 17, 1994): 34-38.

Rutherford, Andrew, *Criminal Justice and the Pursuit of Decency* (Winchester, Waterside Press, 1994).
____, *Growing Out Of Crime* Second Edition (Winchester, Waterside Press, 1993).
____ 'The English Penal Crisis: Paradox and Possibilities' in Roger Rideout and Jeffrey Jowell (eds), *Current Legal Problems 1988* (London, Stevens, 1988), 93-113.
____, *Prisons and the Process of Justice* (Oxford, Oxford University Press, 1986)
____, 'Workshops: Linking the institution and urban area', *Prison Service Journal,* 14 (1973): 1-6.

Robert J Sampson, 'The Community' in James Q Wilson and Joan Petersilia (eds), *Crime* (San Francisco, Institute for Contemporary Studies, 1995), 193-216.

Shinnar, Shlomo and Reuel Shinnar, 'The Effects of the Criminal Justice System on the Control of Crime: A Quantitative Approach', *Law and Society Review*, 9 (1975): 681-611.

Silberman, Charles E *Criminal Violence, Criminal Justice* (New York, Random House, 1978).

Skogan, Wesley G, 'Disorder, crime and Community decline' in Tim Hope and Margaret Shaw, (eds), *Communities and Crime Reduction* (London, HMSO, 1988), 48-61.

Skolnick, Jerome H, 'Are More Jails the Answer?', *Dissent*, 25 (1976): 95-97.

Steenhuis Dato W, 'Over kwaliteit en sturing binnen het strafrechtelijk bedrijf' in A Cachet (ed), *Reorganisatie van de Politie: een tussenbalans* (Arnhem, Gouda, Quint, 1992).
_____, 'Individual Rights and Collective Interests in the Application of the Criminal Law' in Josine Junger-Tas and Irene Sagel-Grande (eds), *Criminology in the 21st Century. A collection of essays presented to Professor Wouter Buikhuizen* (Leuven/Apeldoorn, Garant, 1991), 155-160.
_____, 'Criminal Prosecution in The Netherlands' in J E Hall Williams (ed) *The Role of the Prosecutor* (Aldershot, Gower, 1988).
_____, 'Coherence and Coordination in the Administration of Criminal Justice' in Jan van Dijk, Charles Haffmans, Frits Rüter, Julian Schutte and Simon Stolwijk *Criminal Law in Action An overview of current issues in Western societies* (Deventer, Kluwer Law and Taxation Publishers, 1988), 229-245.
_____, 'Problems of Coordination and Cooperation in Daily Practice Between the Different Agencies of the Criminal Justice System' in *Interactions Within the Criminal Justice System* (Seventeenth Criminological Research Conference, Strasbourg, Council of Europe, 1986), 10-30.
_____, 'Experiences in Police Effectiveness: The Dutch Experience' in R V G Clarke and J M Hughes (eds), *The Effectiveness of Policing* (Aldershot, Gower, 1980), 127-130.
_____, 'Strafrechtelijk Optreden: stapje terug en een sprong voorwaarts' [The working of criminal justice: a small step backward and a huge leap forward] *Delikt en Delinkwent,* 14 (1984): 395-414, 497-512.
_____, and L C M Tigges and J J A Essers, 'The Penal Climate in The Netherlands. Sunny or Cloudy?', *British Journal of Criminology*, 23 (1983): 1-16.

Stolwijk, Simon A M, 'Alternatives to Custodial Sentences' in Jan van Dijk, Charles Haffmans, Frits Rüter, Julian Schutte and Simon Stolwijk (eds), *Criminal Law in Action. An overview of current issues in Western societies* (Deventer, Kluwer Law and Taxation Publishers, 1988), 279-291.

Swaaningen, René van, 'Het confectiepak van product-manager Justitia.' *Recht en Kritkiek* 21 (1995): 13-37.
_____, and Jolande uit Beijerse, 'From Punishment to Diversion and Back Again: The debate on Non-Custodial Sanctions and Penal Reform in the Netherlands', *Howard Journal of Criminal Justice* 32 (1993): 136-156.

144

_____, John Blad and Reinier van Loon, *A Decade of Criminological Research and Penal Policy in the Netherlands; the 1980s: the era of business-management ideology* (Centre for Integrated Penal Sciences, Erasmus University Rotterdam, 1992).

_____, and Gerard de Jonge, 'The Dutch Prison System and Penal Policy in the 1990s. From humanitarian paternalism to penal business management' in Mick Ryan and Vincenzo Ruggierro (eds). *Western European Penal Systems; A Critical Anatomy* (London, Sage, 1995), 24-45.

_____, 'The Moral Revival as Meta-Narrative of Law and Order in the Netherlands for the 1990s' (unpublished paper presented at University of Kent, 1993).

Swart, Bert, and James Young, 'The European Convention on Human Rights and Criminal Justice in the Netherlands and the UK', in Phil Fennnell, Christopher Harding, Nico Jörg and Bert Swart (eds), *Criminal Justice in Europe A Comparative Study* (Oxford, Oxford University Press, 1995), 57-86.

Thatcher, Margaret, *Margaret Thatcher, The Path To Power* (London, Harper Collins, 1995).

Tonry, Michael, *Malign Neglect - Race, Crime and Punishment in America* (New York and Oxford, Oxford University Press, 1995).

_____, 'Mandatory Penalties' in Michael Tonry and Norval Morris (eds), *Crime and Justice, A Review of Research*, (Chicago and London, University of Chicago Press, 1992), 243-273.

Törnudd, Patrik, *Fifteen Years of Decreasing Prisoner Rates in Finland* (Helsinki, National Research Institute of Legal Policy, 1993).

Train, C J, 'The Development of Criminal Policy Planning in the Home Office', *Public Administration,* 55 (1977): 373-384.

Trebach, Arnold S, 'The Loyal Opposition to the War on Drugs' in Jan van Dijk, Charles Haffmans, Frits Rüter, Julian Schutte and Simon Stolwijk (eds), *Criminal Law in Action An overview of current issues in Western Societies* (Deventer, Kluwer Law and Taxation Publishers, 1988), 215-228.

_____, *The Heroin Solution* (New Haven and London, Yale University Press, 1982).

Tuck, Mary, 'Community and the Criminal Justice System', *Policy Studies,* 12 (1991): 22-37.

US Department of Justice, *Prisons and Prisoners in the United States* (Washington, D C, Bureau of Justice Statistics, 1992).

_____, *Attorney General's Summit on Law Enforcement Responses to Violent Crime: Public Safety in the Nineties* Conference Summary (Washington, D C, 1991).

Whitelaw, William, *The Whitelaw Memoirs* (London, Aurum Press, 1989).

Wilson, James Q, 'Crime and Public Policy' in James Q Wilson and Joan Petersilia (eds), *Crime* (San Francisco, Institute for Contemporary Studies, 1995), 489-507.

_____, 'Prisons in a Free Society', *The Public Interest,* 117 (1994): 37-40.

_____, 'Time to Bring Back the Orphanages' *The Sunday Times* (4 December, 1994).

_____, 'In Loco Parentis', *The Brookings Review* (Fall, 1993): 12-15.

_____, *The Moral Sense* (New York, Free Press, 1993).

_____, 'Drugs and Crime' in Michael Tonry and James Q Wilson (eds), *Drugs and Crime* (Chicago and London, University of Chicago Press, 1990), 521-545.

_____, 'On Crime and the Liberals', *Dissent*, 33 (1985): 222-226.

_____, *Thinking About Crime*, Revised edition, (New York, Basic Books, 1983).

_____, (ed), *Crime and Public Policy* (San Francisco, Institute for Contemporary Studies, California, 1983).

_____, 'Crime and American Culture', *The Public Interest*, 70 (1983): 22-48.

_____, '"Policy Intellectuals" and Public Policy', *The Public Interest*, 64 (1981): 31-46.

_____, 'The Political Feasability of Punishment' in J Cederblum and William Blizek (eds), *Justice and Punishment* (Cambridge, Mass, Ballinger, 1977), 107-123.

_____, 'Crime and Punishment in England', *The Public Interest*, 43, (1976): 3-25.

_____, *Thinking About Crime*, (New York, Basic Books, 1975).

_____, 'The Nature and Extent of Crime in the United States' in Marvin R. Summers and Thomas E Barth (eds), *Law and Order in a Democratic Society* (Columbus, Ohio, Charles E Merrill, 1970), 5-15.

_____, *Varieties of Police Behaviour*, (Cambridge, Massachusetts, Harvard University Press, 1968).

_____, *The Amateur Democrat Club Politics in Three Cities* (Chicago and London, University of Chicago Press, Revised edition, 1966).

_____, *Negro Politics, The Search for Leadership* (Glencoe, Ill, Free Press, 1960)

_____, and John J DiIulio, 'Crackdown. Treating the symptoms of the drug problem', *The New Republic*, 201 (1993): 21-25.

_____, and Richard J Herrnstein, *Crime and Human Nature, The definitive study of the causes of crime* (NewYork, Simon and Schuster, 1885).

_____, and George L Kelling, 'Broken Windows: The police and neighbourhood safety', *The Atlantic Monthly,* 249 (1982): 29-38.

_____, and Barbara Boland, 'The Effect of the Police on Crime', *Law and Society Review*, 12 (1978): 367-390.

_____, and Robert L Dupont, 'The Sick Sixties', *The Atlantic Monthly*, 232 (1973): 91-98.

_____, and Mark H Moore and I David Wheat, 'The Problem of Heroin', *The Public Interest*, 29 (1972): 3-28.

Windlesham, Lord, *Responses to Crime, Volume Two, Penal Policy in the Making* (Oxford, Oxford University Press, 1993).

Woolf Report, *Prison Disturbances, April 1990 Report of an Inquiry* by the Rt Hon Lord Justice Woolf (Parts I and II) and His Honour Judge Stephen Tumim (Part II). Cm 1456 (London, HMSO, 1991).

Wolfgang, Marvin, Robert Figlio and Thorsten Sellin, *Delinquency in a Birth Cohort* (Chicago, University of Chicago Press, 1972).

Young, Hugo, *One Of Us, A Biography of Margaret Thatcher* (London, Macmillan, 1989).

Young, Jock, 'Incessant Chatter: Recent Paradigms in Criminology' in Mike Maguire, Rod Morgan and Robert Reiner (eds), *The Oxford Handbook of Criminology* (Oxford, Oxford University Press, 1994), 69-124.

Zimring, Franklin E, and Gordon Hawkins, *Incapacitation. Penal Confinement and the Restraint of Crime* (New York and Oxford, Oxford University Press, 1995).

____, 'The Growth of Imprisonment in California', *British Journal of Criminology*, 34 (1994): 83-96.

____,*Prison Population and Criminal Justice Policy in California* (Institute of Governmental Studies, Berkeley, University of California Press, 1992).

____, *The Scale of Imprisonment* (Chicago and London, University of Chicago Press, 1991).

Index

Centenary of Dutch Criminal Code
(1986) conference 68-70
Dato Steenhuis' speech 68-70

Chaiken, Marcia R and Jan M 54n.85

Children and Young Persons Act
1933 (England and Wales) 101

Christie, Nils
warning on criminal policy in US
126
'joint moral community' 129-131,
133
vulnerability of tolerance 133,
135n.6

Clark, Ramsey, U.S. Attorney,
general, exponent of liberal criminal
policy 26, 50n.44

Clarke, Ronald V G 122n.59

Clarke, Kenneth, Home Secretary
127-128

Clinton, Bill, Administration stance
on criminal policy 135n.1

Cloward, Richard A 24, 47n.9

Cohen, Jacqueline 51n.60, 54n.88

Conservative Party manifesto (1987)
99, 120n.38

Council of Europe, Criminological
Research Seminar (1986),
contribution of Dato Steenhuis 70-71

Cressey, Donald R 24, 49n.34

Crime Commission (President's
Commission on Law Enforcement and
the Administration of Justice, 1965-
67,*The Challenge of Crime in a Free
Society*)
established by President Johnson 19
liberal vision of criminal policy
20-21, 23

leitmotif rejected by James Q
Wilson 15, 24
support of community-based
sentencing 29, 47ns.1, 12, 49n.31,
81n.24

Crime and Human Nature, co-authors
James Q Wilson and Richard J
Herrnstein 29

*Crime, Justice and Protecting the
Public* (England and Wales, white
paper, 1990) 100, 104-106, 121n.50

Crime Policy Planning Unit (England
and Wales) 85

Criminal Justice: A Working Paper
(England and Wales, 1984) 93,
120n.29

Criminal Justice Act 1982 (England
and Wales) 89, 100, 107, 118n.22,
119n.31

Criminal Justice Act 1988 (England
and Wales) 106

Criminal Justice Act 1991 (England
and Wales) 100, 115-116, 126-127,
123n.67

Criminal Justice Act 1993 (England
and Wales) 128

Criminal Justice and Public Order Act
1994 (England and Wales) 128

Criminal policy,
definitions 11-12
as a dynamic process 12
absence of new foundations 12-13
and normative concepts 13
debasement of, in United States
44-46
Steenhuis' analogy with
commercial enterprise 62-64
Society and Crime, as first national
statement of Dutch criminal policy
65-68
Netherlands in the 1990s 125

152

Haag, Ernest van den 48n.23

Haan, Willem de 77ns.2, 3, 79n.32

Hart, Auguste C 't
criminal law policy 12, 61
crisis in confidence in Dutch
criminal justice 60
OM's emerging policy-making role
60
critique of *Society and Crime* 67
Law in Motion 72-73
Steenhuis 71
Strafrecht met beleid 73
16n.4, 17n.8, 77n.9, 78n.22, 80n.44

Hare, David 121n.47

Hawkins, Gordon 40, 51n.66,
54ns.94, 95, 136n.27

Hecklo, Hugh 50n.52

Herrnstein, Richard J, collaboration
with James Q Wilson 29, 45, 51n.57,
57n.140

Heymann, Philip 11, 16n.1

Hirsch, Andrew von
critique of incapacitation theory 36
James Q Wilson's influence on
mandatory prison sentencing
statutes 37, 54n.91, 121n.42

Hirschi, Travis 53n.80

Home Office (England and Wales)
Research and Planning Unit 85,
111
'special conferences' 90, 119n.25
seminar at Leeds Castle (1987)
99-100, 105, 112

Hood, Roger 50n.55

Hope, Tim 122n.60

Howard, Michael, Home Secretary
128, 135n.9

Howard League for Penal Reform 87,
91, 105, 136n.26

Humphries D 17n.14

Hurd, Douglas, Home Secretary 86,
90, 97, 99, 103, 107, 120n.37, 40,
121n.48

Huling, Tracy 55n.110

Incapacitation theory
critique by Andrew von
Hirsch 36
RAND Corporation study
34-36
assessment by David Faulkner 98

Institute for the Study and Treatment
of Delinquency (ISTD) 105

Johnson, President Lyndon B
Crime Commission 19-20
Administration policy and illegal
drugs 38

Jones, Carol, managerialism and
absence of principled policy 134,
136n.29

Jonge, G de 76, 18n.17, 78n.17

Jung, Heike 17n.7

Junger-Tas, Josine 79n.33

'just deserts' 100, 103-104

Juvenile justice and young offenders,
England 101-102, 105,
106-107, 127, 122n.53, 54
USA 33

Katzenbach, Nicholas, US Attorney
General 19

Kelk, Constantijn
Utrecht School 61, 63
definition of *belied* (policy) 60

153

157

'war on drugs' and young black Americans 40
debasement of criminal policy in US 44, 50n. 48, 54n. 96, 56n.114, 57n.138

Törnudd, Patrik, criminal policy in Finland 129-130, 118n.14, 136ns.16, 18

Train, C J 117n.3

Trebach, Arnold 39, 55n.102

Trevelyan, Denis 88

Tuck, Mary 120n.34, 122n.60

Tulkens, Hans 118n.14

Turner, Susan 54n.90

United Nations Congress on the Prevention of Crime and the Treatment of Offenders
(1985) 114
(1990) 95

United States Sentencing Commission, drugs sentencing policy 39

Upton (1980) 119n.31

Utrecht School 59-60

Victims of crime, England 113-114

Visher, Christy A, reanalysis of RAND study 36, 54n.88

Vorenberg, James, 49n.31

Waddington, David, Home Secretary 86, 105-105

Wheat, David I 55n.103

Whitelaw, William, Home Secretary 86, 88-90, 106
attempts to reduce prison

population 88-90, 118ns.17, 19, 20, 121n.38

Wickersham Commission 33

Wilberforce, Lord 97

Wiles, Paul 43, 57n.130

Wilson, James Q
hard-edged approach to criminal policy 15
adviser to the Crime Commission 20-21
rejection of Crime Commission leitmotif 15, 24
education and early career 21-22
president of American Political Science Association 21
chair of National Advisory Council on Drug Abuse Prevention 38
prolific publications 22-23
criminal policy, a 'we-they' vision 23-24
popular and elite beliefs 24-26
conservative and liberal differences 26-29, 31-32
influence of intellectuals 26-27
and values of a free society 36
wholehearted endorsement of imprisonment 23-24, 29-30
deterrence theory 30-37
incapacitation theory 30
influence of the Shinnars' study 30-31
'career criminals' 34-35
RAND Corporation research 34-36
dismissal of critics 36
use of research findings 37
critique of *Principles of Criminology and Delinquency and Opportunity* 24
policy and causal analysis 24
sober view of man 25-26
Massachusetts Task Force on Juvenile Crime 29
Reagan Administration's Task Force on Violent Crime 29, 32-34
juvenile justice and 'career criminals' 33
and arrest records 37

Some further titles from Waterside Press

Growing Out of Crime The New Era Andrew Rutherford A classic and challenging work about young offenders and their progress towards adulthood. (Second reprint) ISBN 1 872 870 06 6. £12.

Criminal Justice and the Pursuit of Decency Andrew Rutherford
'By reminding us that, without "good men and women" committed to humanising penal practice, criminal justice can so easily sink into apathy and pointless represssion, Andrew Rutherford has sounded both a warning and a note of optimism.': *Sunday Telegraph.* ISBN 1 872 870 21 X. £12.50.

Criminal Classes Offenders at School Angela Devlin As featured by the BBC and in *The Guardian*, this book examines for the first time in detail the links between educational failure and offending. ISBN 1 872 870 30 9. £16.

Introduction to the **Criminal Justice Process** Bryan Gibson Paul Cavadino 'Rarely, if ever, has this complex process been described with such comprehensiveness and clarity, total lack of jargon and in a mere 160 pages': *Justice of the Peace.* ISBN 1 872 870 09 0. £12.

Introduction to the **Magistrates' Court** Bryan Gibson The second edition of this popular work. A clear and comprehensive outline in twelve concise chapters - plus a *Glossary of Words, Phrases and Abbreviations* (750 entries). ISBN 1 872 870 15 5. £10.

Introduction to the **Probation Service** Anthony Osler An illuminating overview, including a brief history and a survey of modern-day duties, responsibilities and issues. ISBN 1 872 870 19 8. £10.

The Sentence of the Court A Handbook for Magistrates Michael Watkins, Winston Gordon and Anthony Jeffries. Consultant Dr David Thomas. Foreword by Lord Taylor, Lord Chief Justice. Created under the auspices of the Justices' Clerks' Society, the handbook has been supplied to every magistrate in areas such as Inner London, Manchester, Bristol and Newcastle. This invaluable guide for *all* practitioners contains a simple but effective outline of magistrates' sentencing powers. ISBN 1 872 870 25 2. £10.

Order direct from WATERSIDE PRESS, Domum Road, Winchester, S023 9NN. Tel or Fax 01962 855567. The direct mail price is given above. **Important:** please add £1.50 per volume for p&p to a maximum of £6 (UK only. Postage abroad is charged at cost). Cheques should be made payable to 'Waterside Press'. If requested, we can invoice organizations for two or more books.